Visual Controls

Applying Visual Management to the Factory

Visual Controls

Applying Visual Management to the Factory

Chris A. Ortiz
Murry R. Park

CRC Press
Taylor & Francis Group
Boca Raton   London   New York

CRC Press is an imprint of the
Taylor & Francis Group, an **informa** business

A PRODUCTIVITY PRESS BOOK

Productivity Press
Taylor & Francis Group
270 Madison Avenue
New York, NY 10016

© 2011 by Taylor and Francis Group, LLC
Productivity Press is an imprint of Taylor & Francis Group, an Informa business

No claim to original U.S. Government works

Printed in the United States of America on acid-free paper
10 9 8 7 6 5 4 3 2 1

International Standard Book Number: 978-1-4398-2090-2 (Paperback)

Library of Congress Cataloging-in-Publication Data

Ortiz, Chris A.
 Visual controls : applying visual management to the factory / Chris A. Ortiz, Murry Park.
  p. cm.
 Includes index.
 ISBN 978-1-4398-2090-2 (pbk. : alk. paper)
 1. Production management. 2. Visual communication. 3. Manufacturing processes.
I. Park, Murry. II. Title.

TS155.O775 2011
658.5--dc22
                    2010044864

Visit the Taylor & Francis Web site at
http://www.taylorandfrancis.com

and the Productivity Press Web site at
http://www.productivitypress.com

Contents

Introduction

From the dawn of civilization, people have been sending *visual* signals to one another; from smoke signals sent into the horizon from a primitive campfire to sophisticated communication signals regulated by advanced control systems, we humans have a long history of using visual means to communicate significant information to one another. In fact, visual communication is in play all around us, performing a critical role in today's fast-paced society. Even though visual communication systems are abundant elsewhere in our lives, however, the benefits of effective visual control systems are not yet commonly realized in manufacturing organizations around the world.

In our everyday lives, we negotiate our way through each day, in part by following the signs, symbols, images, and colors intended to communicate key information as we commute, transact, and carry out our daily activities. Many visual signals are created to influence and, at times, to control thought processes, thereby influencing the resulting physical actions. In most cases, the visual signal is presented in a way that is intended to get one's immediate attention and to prompt some type of action. Oftentimes, visual controls are accompanied by a set of audible controls. Together, visual and audible controls can be key players in achieving desired human behavior, not only in our everyday lives but also in business.

This book considers the application of various visual control methods that collectively make up the company's greater visual management system.

VISUAL CONTROLS IN SOCIETY

Some primary drivers for implementing visual control systems in the twenty-first century society include the following:

- Improved safety
  - Improving synchronized movement of automobiles and pedestrians (traffic intersections, crosswalks, school zones)

- Communicating the presence of construction zones and providing a means for safe passage
- Superior communication
  - Aiding travelers at airports as they attempt to safely negotiate parking, baggage check-in, and movement to departure gates, including passage through security
  - Painted lines, arrows, and footprints on surfaces to indicate direction of motion
  - Restroom gender indicators
- Better security
  - In airport terminals: symbols indicating contraband, wrong-way, and controlled-access areas
  - In military installations: indicators as to where one can safely proceed, use of controlled nametags, and signage at secure or controlled areas
  - At business entrances: controlled access into secure areas, painted walkways to alert people to stay clear of operating equipment, and posted placards
  - In secure work zones: cones, colored tape, security guards, and warning signage
  - In unsafe areas: safety cones, signs, barriers, and tape
- Recognition of law enforcement and emergency vehicles
  - Flashing lights
  - Flares
- Human interfaces to devices
  - ATMs
  - Computers
  - Cell phones and personal digital assistants (PDAs)
  - Production equipment controls
  - Light switches
- Advertising
  - In stores
  - Posted on billboards
  - On product labeling
- Internet advertising

VISUAL CONTROL SYSTEMS AT CROSSWALKS

One relatively simple example of a visual control system in society is the use of visual control signals at a street's intersection. As part of a city's effort to provide for synchronized and safe traffic and pedestrian flow, a crosswalk is marked and controlled to reduce pedestrian–car accidents and near misses. The crosswalk indicator is just one subcomponent of the intersection's larger visual control system. The system may consist of a controller, software, hardware and wiring, inputs (switches), and outputs (indicators such as turn arrows and red, amber, and green lights). Crosswalks typically have signage and are marked to indicate *where* safe passage of the street may occur. As a part of the larger system, the crosswalk light itself is used as a visual indicator, or "control," to indicate *when* it is safe or unsafe to move across the crosswalk. When time to enter or cross the crosswalk is getting short to make safe passage to the other side, the light may start blinking, may show a countdown timer, or may change color. When it is not safe to use the crosswalk, a combination of symbology and colors, such as the symbol of a blinking raised red hand, specifies that information.

Crosswalk visual control systems have evolved right along with the number of cars, trucks, and people. Ongoing changes in traffic and parking laws, the increasing diversity of people living and working together (culture and language), and the worldwide movement toward greener vehicle technologies suggest that the level of complexity of these systems is evolving as well.

The crosswalk is a simple example of how visual controls are used to help prevent accident or injury, which is clearly a safety initiative (and perhaps also an attempt to avoid liability should an accident occur). Whatever combination of symbology and lighting is used, as a society we learn, adapt, and adjust our behavior to accommodate the visual controls used within the pedestrian and traffic control systems. We can use similar systems in our businesses to provide enormous safety and mistake-proofing benefits.

VISUAL CONTROLS IN ADVERTISING

Another example of the use of visual controls is found in advertising. Rather than an attempt to control security or to provide a safer environment, the visual signs of advertising are attempts to present a message and to get people to buy in to an idea, a product, or a service. Whether seen on a billboard, a television commercial, or the latest Internet "pop-up" ad, these visual controls are intended to secure our attention, if, but for a moment, to:

- Influence our minds regarding the concept being presented
- Manipulate our thinking toward the purchase of a product or service
- Suggest our involvement in donating to a charity
- Ask for our participation in a political movement

VISUAL CONTROLS IN BUSINESS

In business, this same type of visual advertising is used to send or reinforce a message or to influence employees to embrace a concept or new direction management wishes to communicate.

Even though much is yet to be learned about the way the human brain interprets what the eyes see, one thing is clear: what our eyes do see— and the processing that follows in the vast wiring of our minds—happens immediately and normally secures our attention long enough to modify our behavior.

The limited use of visual controls in manufacturing operations around the world today stands in stark contrast to the successful implementation elsewhere in our society. Some manufacturing companies have implemented pockets of visual controls or have made a half-hearted attempt. In many production operations, the existing visual control systems are the equivalent of having a crosswalk without having any crosswalk controls in place—that is, low on the evolutionary trajectory.

VISUAL CONTROLS IN MANUFACTURING

Why don't we see a greater use of visual control systems in current manufacturing operations? We have concluded that management does not understand the benefits of such a system or does not know how to design and implement one. In Chapter 1, we will review the benefits of using visual controls in a production operation. The remaining chapters convey the "how to" of designing and implementing a successful visual management system.

Controlling the flow of product is very similar to controlling the flow of vehicular traffic. The same combination of elements—demand (movement of product rather than automobiles), people, evolving technologies, and increasingly diverse human demographics—presents similar challenges in both environments. In manufacturing, the accidents or near misses come in the form of nonconforming product, late deliveries, and cost overruns. The need for timely information coupled with desired human behavior is as critical to the competitive survival of a manufacturing operation as it is to the safety of pedestrians at a crosswalk—perhaps even more so.

As discussed already, visual controls in a manufacturing facility may be designed to support a company-wide safety initiative or to advertise a strategic business initiative to the workforce. However, an even more important justification for implementing a visual control system is the potential to achieve the proper flow of product, and the balanced consumption and movement of inventory and use of resources, throughout the operation. The net results are as follows:

- Production employees waste less time waiting.
- More timely, correct decisions can be made on the production floor.
- Improvement of first-pass quality and reduction of rework.
- Lower work-in-process levels.
- Lower purchased inventory levels.

Companies that develop a visual control system to deliver timely, accurate, and appropriate information to the employees working in the process enjoy a heightened level of performance, fewer wasted actions, and improved profitability. This is no secret. When presented with simple (the simpler the better), accurate, and timely information, employees can make better and more timely decisions. The "control" part of visual control suggests that information is communicated in a timely manner to signal, aid, suggest, or influence human behavior. This, in turn, improves productivity, quality, and delivery performance. A successful visual control system not only can complement other Lean initiatives but also can provide another competitive edge.

The use of visual controls is no panacea; it is, nevertheless, a critical tool to leverage in an organization's quest to operate at the highest level in this increasingly global economy. Visual controls do more than simply communicate nice-to-know information for an employee or a team. Creating a visual control system takes cross-functional planning and implementation to provide those few critical pieces of information and to present them at the right process step, at the right time, and to the right person or team in a visual and easily understood manner.

VISUAL CONTROLS AND THE EIGHT WASTES

As Lean practitioners and teachers, we know the power of the visual factory and how it can become the platform for further improvement. The concept of visual controls is a major part of a Lean manufacturing system, which focuses on waste reduction. Developing, sustaining, and improving on a visual factory will result in the removal or reduction of a significant amount of waste. Many readers already understand the concepts of *waste* and *Lean*. For those of you just getting started, here is a brief description of the eight categories of waste found in any operation. (Note that *Lean* traditionally defines seven categories of waste, but the eighth category is often added nowadays.)

1. Overproduction: the act of making more product than necessary or of completing it faster than necessary—before it is needed. Overproduced product takes up floor space, requires handling and storage, and could result in potential quality problems if the lot was made wrong.
2. Overprocessing: the practice of taking extra steps, of rechecking, reverifying, and overperforming the work. This often occurs in fabrication departments when sanding, deburring, cleaning, or polishing is overdone because the required finished state is not specified and visible to the operator. Machines can also overprocess when they are not maintained properly because maintenance problems are not visible.
3. Waiting: occurs when important information, tools, and supplies are not readily available, causing machines and people to be idle. Imbalances in workloads and cycle times between processes can also cause waiting.

4. Waiting motion: the movement of people, often when they are look-ing for things. Where are my tools? Where are my parts? Where is the work instruction?

5. Transportation: the movement of parts and product throughout the facility. Often requiring a forklift, hand truck, or pallet jack, trans-portation occurs when consuming processes are far away from each other and are not visible.

6. Inventory: waste when manufacturers tie up too much money holding excessive levels of raw, work-in-process, and finished-goods inventory.

7. Defects: any quality deficiency that causes scrap, warranty claims, or rework hours because of mistakes made in the factory.

8. Wasted human potential: not properly using employees to the best of their abilities. People can be only as successful as the limits of the process they are given to work in allow them to be. If a process inher-ently involves motion, transportation, overprocessing, overproduc-tion, periods of waiting, and defect creation, then that is exactly how people will be able to perform.

A visual factory can help you reduce or even eliminate these eight wastes and by doing so to create a much more productive and profitable company for all.

This book was written with a flow that allows you to understand the concept of visual controls from the macro level of overall business infra-structure requirements, plant layout, work area and department setup down to visual tools and parts and visual communication. Our hope is that you will read this book and not just be inspired but also able to roll up your sleeves and begin the journey toward an effective visual manage-ment system.

Acknowledgments

Foremost, I would like thank my wife, Pavlina, and my beautiful young boys, Sebastian and Samuel. Family support to any business owner and author is an absolute requirement for success. They have endured my monthly business trips and countless hours alone while I was busy writing this manuscript.

My staff at Kaizen Assembly was integral in helping me complete my part of the manuscript. I have to thank John Elkins and Patricia Brunhirl for their efforts in developing figures and ensuring that Murry and I had the support needed to keep writing.

I would also like to thank Murry for his assistance as he helped start most of the chapters and provided a fantastic lead-in to my style of writing. This is my first coauthored book, and his contribution and teamwork were inspiring on many levels.

Taylor & Francis published my very first book, *Kaizen Assembly: Designing, Constructing, and Managing a Lean Assembly Line.* I appreciate their trust in me as a writer and must thank them for yet another endeavor together. Finally, the people I meet and assist throughout my travels as a consultant equally deserve my thanks. I learn so much from them, and their eagerness for excellence and continuous improvement only makes me a better advisor for them. I have the utmost respect for every one of them.

Chris Ortiz

Coauthoring this book with Chris proved to be a unique and beneficial experience. His industry knowledge and practical insight proved invaluable as we pulled the concepts together. Also, his uncanny ability to boil technical concepts down into understandable, bite-size pieces was quite helpful.

Thanks, too, to Shelley, my wife, for providing me with countless hours of solitude—and support—as I attempted to succinctly capture and organize these thoughts, visual management examples, and experiences into a palatable manuscript.

Murry Park

1

Importance of the Visual Factory

Many owners, senior executives, and midlevel managers claim that their company's products and the highly tuned (and sometimes extremely expensive) manufacturing equipment they operate are quite different from other operations; in fact, they claim that they are unique. The argument often follows that the concepts of *Lean, formal quality systems,* or *visual controls* might work for everyone else, but these ideas and methods simply do not apply in their factory. The uniqueness of their company is most often absolutely valid—which implies that they have a distinct competitive advantage.

THE COMMON GROUND OF PRODUCTION ENVIRONMENTS

However, no matter how unique a company's position, there is still common ground shared by all production environments regardless of the specific company or product. This common ground manifests in the form of *people, processes,* and *inventory.* Wherever people are employed, processes are used, and inventory is stored and moved, an opportunity to create positive change through visual communication and visual controls exists, regardless of the product, service, or process in use. In manufacturing operations, the successful combination of visual communication and visual controls is referred to as the visual factory.

A properly designed visual control system helps keep waste—once known as "hidden costs"—off the production floor and underscores the importance of identifying and exploiting opportunities to remove waste. Not only do visual indicators help us become leaner; they also keep our focus on items that otherwise fall back into obscurity.

For the analytical executive, who requires a quantitative return on investment prior to launching into any Lean initiative, including a visual control system, please note: the benefits of implementing such a system are not based on fuzzy numbers. Creating a proper foundation for a visual control system relies heavily on the scientific method. Likewise, the results are "scientific": companies commonly report staggering cost, quality, and productivity improvements, with productivity improvements often reported in the double digits or higher.

People

Regardless of whether your company manufactures a complex aerospace component or a simple commodity item, people are intimately involved in designing, planning, producing, inspecting, and testing products. These individuals are essential to ensuring that the company meets cost, quality, and delivery commitments. The need to have people on board is the first reason that a visual control system warrants consideration by management personnel.

The combination of the human brain and hand working together is a great example of a multiaxis manipulator, but the triple combination of the human eye, brain, and hand may be the ultimate instance of sensing (eye), discerning (brain), and doing (hand). Unlike a sensor that simply indicates the status of a variable on a piece of equipment, the human eye can capture, the mind can process, and the hands can react quickly to the information received. Unlike a sensor, the human mind will evaluate, sometimes incorrectly, the information provided. The imperfect nature of the human mind suggests the need for simplicity, training, and retraining when learning a new process. Therefore, whatever signals we ask the human eye to recognize and mind to process, they must be simple, clear, and concise, leaving no doubt as to the desired follow-on action.

Manufacturing managers must also consider the impact of the "cowboy effect"; that is, the effect of employees who are rugged, hard-working, intelligent, and very independent men and women on the production floor. These are the folks who may have 20 years' seniority, are highly skilled and very productive, rely on little documentation, and "just know" how to do their jobs. They are also the keepers of production's undocumented tribal knowledge.

It is not that they have absolute disdain for anyone trying to tell them how to approach their work differently; it is just a little hard for them to be completely receptive. These folks equate producing a product to riding a spirited bronco. There may be a few basic ground rules to follow, but do not go telling a cowboy how to stay on a bucking horse unless you have done it yourself—and recently.

In manufacturing processes, whereas independent thinking is great, independent actions are not. Achieving predictable and desirable results in a production environment requires that we set aside the cowboy (or cowgirl) in each of us and subordinate ourselves to the success of the process—the one we are there to operate and support. Although society usually applauds individualism, manufacturing's need for predictability and certainty is paramount. That predictability relies on good planning, reliable material availability, skilled and punctual workers, reliable and calibrated equipment, and precise process control.

Finally, when we employ people, we have ample opportunity to experience poor communication. Incomplete, inaccurate, and untimely communication is a major source of waste on the production floor. Furthermore, with more workers speaking English as a second language, the need for clear communication is even more critical in U.S. manufacturing.

When we couple the tendency for humans to make mistakes with the independence-prone American psyche and the opportunities for miscommunication in any organization, we can see that we have our work cut out for us. Although a visual management system is not the answer to all the company's challenges regarding human tendencies, the system can help address these challenges and can even leverage employees' strengths.

Processes

A process is a process is a process. Life is a process. Sales is a process, too. So are research, engineering, finance, order creation, design, master scheduling, planning, procurement, production, testing, quality, safety, legal, and environmental activities. A manufacturing process may be patented with no one outside the company having any knowledge of it, yet it is still a process with inputs, outputs, and something that occurs in between. If it is a unique process, the inputs, outputs, and creative steps that take place in between are what make it different. However, the following items are common to all processes:

- Time (process time and setup or changeover time)
- Human interfaces (e.g., hiring, training, and communication)
- Impact of engineering changes, expedites, and nonconforming incoming raw materials and components

So, how would any given process benefit from the use of visual controls? Let's start by breaking down how visual controls can affect the common process items.

Time

- Processing time: The time it takes the process to add value to the end product. Visual indicators showing the operational status of the process, especially when an unplanned event occurs, can shave seconds or minutes off response times, ultimately helping to optimize process uptime and increase capacity. Visual signals can also be used to speed up repair, startup, and adjustment of the process, thereby reducing unplanned downtime.
- Setup or changeover time: These activities are a version of planned downtime. Visual indicators can help reduce setup or changeover time. One example is a timer that starts counting down once the machine has completed its cycle. The timer, which is a visual signal (sometimes accompanied by an audible signal), is a call for attention, which means all assigned employees are to converge upon the setup activity and complete the nonvalue-added sequence in short order according to a defined procedure to allow the restart of production. The visual countdown timer is also a measurement of performance to the standard, fostering healthy coworker peer pressure to perform in the time expected. Visual controls can aid in expediting the external and internal steps both before and during the setup or changeover event.

Human Interfaces

- Training: It can cost quite a bit to train a new employee. Using company- and process-specific symbols, signs, colors, and other simple visual methods to aid in the training process can help complete successful training more quickly and effectively.
- Communication: Visualize this scenario: The production supervisor or manager is in a meeting when a question arises in manufacturing as to what part to start next. Someone says there has been a change to the production plan because of a shift in priorities. Production staff members interrupt the meeting and have the manager step into the hall for a minute. Worse yet, they wait until the meeting is over to find out that the change had, indeed, occurred. Even worse, they

follow the original plan only to find out after the meeting they are now making the wrong parts. Somehow the information was not passed along to the operator who needed to know it. In the meantime, a setup or changeover was spent, material was consumed, and product was produced that was no longer needed. Conversely, the presentation of accurate and timely visual information can prevent such uncertainty.

- Training example, assembly line: Although trained and certified to operate the assembly line station, an assembler is unclear how to proceed with a new product coming down the line. There are written instructions in the form of a controlled document, but the wording is confusing. So, the assembler leaves her workstation to get further clarification. This is an example of an appropriate place to use visual controls in work instructions to help anyone assigned to complete the task.

- Communication example, equipment: How many times have we heard, "I lost my ability to think for a minute," after identifying a problem? One company actually had a term it used for capturing such an event as a causal code in its quality system. However, the use of simple colors and symbols can greatly enhance, and simplify, a machine operator's job. Switches or any input required by the operator and lights or any output to be recognized by the operator can be visual and simple.

Engineering Changes, Expediting, and Nonconforming Product

- Imagine this scenario: A machinist has just started producing a part following the usual specifications. He does not know that an engineering change order had been issued earlier in the morning effective "ASAP," because somehow he just did not get the word. Every process is subject to changes in both product and process specifications. Alerting the production floor visually of pending specification changes can emphasize the change and prevent catastrophic mishaps.

- Why does a company expedite? Is there ever a good reason to turn a production floor upside down with a "hot off the press" plan that stops the flow of product, increases work in process (WIP), increases downtime, steals from inventory, and frustrates employees? Normally, it is simply poor planning on the part of your sales and marketing department or a customer. Many managers fail to recognize the waste, costs, and disservice to staff and customer of allowing the expediting process to continue. A Lean operation uses the expedite process as a rare exception, if at all. Knowing that expedites will rarely occur, managers can use visual means to help deal with the chaos and minimize the collateral damage that follows.

- What is the bottom-line impact to your business every time a nonconforming product is allowed to enter the factory with the intent of being consumed into a saleable product? Why do we ever let nonconforming raw material, components, or subassemblies reach our production floors? The resultant waste of time, material, and effort is often enormous. Visual controls can help ensure that only product known to be good makes its way into the factory. And what happens when a defect is created in a process? The use of visual controls can stop further production of bad parts, can quarantine nonconforming product, can identify obsolete documentation, and can ensure that when the time comes to start producing again the results will be predictably favorable.

Inventory

For some manufacturing executives, the more inventory sitting on the shelf, the more secure they feel about their business. However, business managers who carry more inventory than what is required to meet customer demand have a false sense of security, because extra inventory is more likely hiding problems that will surface later. For the purposes of this chapter, we will break inventory into the three stages of raw materials, work in process (WIP), and finished goods.

Raw Materials

What are our inventory levels? A modern enterprise resource planning (ERP) system can keep track of it all, including forecasting, master scheduling, planning, inventory, min–max quantities, and reorder quantities. The bottom line, though, is this: When do we need parts, and how many do we need? A simple visual "pull" system can be used to effectively manage supplies of parts and consumables.

WIP Levels

- Where should your factory's WIP level be? In a Lean company, the ideal WIP level is the amount of product undergoing a value-added process only—and not one item more. In the real world, however, companies that are implementing Lean manufacturing find they still need to count nonvalue-added WIP steps in their equation. Visual controls can help keep a better handle on WIP levels.

Finished Goods

- How are finished goods organized? Are they arranged in a first-in–first-out system? How would one know? A visual controls system can help.

The Bottom Line—Making Information Accessible

Manufacturing companies that use people and processes and carry inventories are faced with common challenges, and the implementation of visual controls can aid in better meeting commitments to customers.

It is no secret that seeing really is believing. Without giving it much thought, what we see often dictates how we respond—both mentally and physically. And, in a nutshell, that's the whole idea. Successful implementation of a visual control system takes advantage of the power of a person's ability to see, comprehend, and react in a desirable and timely manner.

Visual controls in manufacturing are simply a means of presenting key business, product, and process information in such a way that it is "visible" at the right time, in the right place, to the right employees, throughout the factory. Sharing information in e-mails, on bulletin boards, in meetings, or on Web sites where only a select few have access and the timing of the communication is random is marginally effective. On the other hand, visual control systems hone in on a proven form of human communication as old as the campfire smoke signal: that is, what we see—right in front of us—while we are working in a process. For production workers, the presence of visual controls means that the information needed to make the best decisions for the company in a given area is right here, right now.

MANAGEMENT'S ROLE

As many times as we have seen the light shine in the eyes of owners and senior executives who embrace Lean concepts, we have also encountered those who simply do not see the merit in supporting Lean initiatives;

oftentimes they give only lip service to what they perceive as a trendy business concept that will pass with time. Managers who introduce and implement some of these concepts incorrectly may experience failure.

However, those who properly embrace Lean strategies, including implementing a visual control system, will see positive change. Managers must engage in Lean strategy-setting meetings that lead to in-depth training of all employees. As employees learn about and practice Lean manufacturing concepts, they and their managers begin to embrace the new culture that emerges—a culture that reflects the importance of education and leverages the minds and intuition of the whole group. Everyone begins to simplify, to break down the complicated and cumbersome systems of days gone by. The creation of meaningful visual indicators becomes second nature.

This new business paradigm relies on mutual trust. The simplest way to kill a Lean initiative is to micromanage it. The best way to reap the benefits of Lean is simply to step back and let go, once production workers are trained to comprehend and practice Lean correctly.

THE BASICS OF THE VISUAL FACTORY: 5S

A 5S initiative is often the springboard for launching a visual management system. The 5S's—sort, set in order, scrub or shine, standardize, and sustain—represent a systematic approach to cleaning and organizing a work area. The basic concept of 5S is straightforward and easy to understand, but its implementation can be a little harder. Often, professionals learning about the visual factory think that 5S represents the entirety of a visual management system. However, although 5S is indeed key in organizing work areas and represents a very important element of the visual factory, it is just an introduction to the potential role a visual management system can play.

Labeling the production floor, walls, workbenches, tools, shelves, and totes brings a microvisual management system into play. When we sort, we are systematically removing unneeded items from the work area. Setting in order takes the remaining items (equipment, workbenches, tools, documentation) and floor space and organizes it all (e.g., labeling the floor, workbenches, tool boards, and tools) in a way that best supports the value-added operations within the work area. After the area is scrubbed or shined, the best standardized processes are identified or created and documented. This includes involving key "experts" to capture (document) the best practice and then training everyone on the new way of doing things. The last S is for sustaining the previous four S's. 5S is described in further detail in Chapter 2.

Whereas the 5S concept is focused on organizing a production area to optimize how value is added to a product, a visual management system is an interactive system used to monitor and assist in providing the desired companywide value stream. This includes visually reporting the flow of product, with supporting information, encompassing everything from raw materials through to finished goods. In other words, the visual control system provides a holistic view of the entire production process and a means of actively managing the flow of product and information throughout.

VISUAL FACTORY LAYOUT

After completing 5S in all areas, a facility is primed for adding components of a visual control system. We start with the visual layout. Proper layout of the facility is critical to the long-term success of the visual management system. Even without a visual factory, a smart layout incorporating good communication and flow of information and product is essential to long-term survival in manufacturing. Unfortunately, inefficient plant layouts are a common problem in many manufacturing environments. Companies often position machines, departments, and processes based solely on available space or where the appropriate facility attributes happen to be located. People often avoid the up-front effort to set up a work area or even a facility properly. Making the effort to do it right first is far more beneficial than the expensive cost of years of motion, transportation, and lack of visibility.

Process-based plant layouts separate internal customers within a value stream and are not conducive to visual management. Each process area or "department" (e.g., grinding, sanding, assembly, drilling, packaging) is separated by long distances, adding waste. When processes are separated by distance, the next customer in the value chain is not visible, and the product must be stored, moved, stored, and moved again before the next value-added process begins (Figure 1.1).

Check Your Reasoning

While conducting a kaizen event, I encountered a useful example of the type of reasoning that can result in inefficient layouts. The kaizen team was actually focusing on improving the layout of the packaging and labeling line. The team came up with what they thought was a good layout to reduce motion and transportation and to promote good communication between workers. After hours of debating, the team presented a new layout. Interestingly, their recommendations actually increased walking and the movement of parts. They had placed the workbenches and machines near the retainer poles securing the building. I commented on the excessive amount of floor space they intended to use and the extent of increased movement.

The reasoning behind the changes was that the outlets for power and air ran down the poles, so that was where the items had to go. They expressed concern that maintenance would have to spend a couple of hours rerouting wires and air lines to accommodate a different layout.

Lean and visual layouts take into account the concept of internal customers. Figure 1.2 shows an example taking the same process and converting to a visual layout that encourages even flow. Chapter 3 discusses an approach to creating a visual factory layout.

VISUAL TOOLS

Once the overall layout of the work areas and the factory has been determined, the detail of each area can be addressed. Tools are required everywhere in a factory. Shipping, receiving, maintenance, research and development, storerooms, equipment, assembly areas, packing lines, warehouse, and quality control all require tools to perform work. Chapter 4 covers visual tools in greater detail, but following are some introductory concepts to ponder.

Tools must be visible, period. There are only a few exceptions, such as expensive calibration devices and similar tools that can be affected by dust.

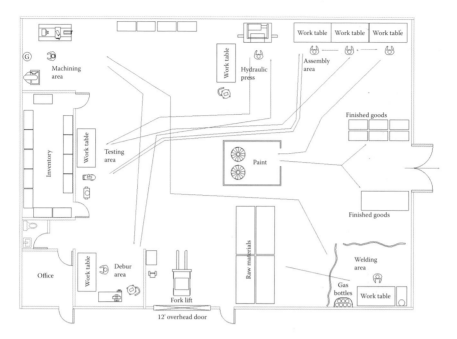

FIGURE 1.1
Nonvisual layout.

Managers and supervisors can be quite nervous about presenting tools visually, because they fear that they will be stolen. However, if stealing is going on, it usually involves a very small percentage of the work force, and that small minority should not be allowed to interfere with your improvement goals.

Tools need to be readily available and in good working condition. Storing necessary tools in a pile, behind a door, in a cabinet, or with broken or unused tools does not meet the requirements of visual management. You must break down these physical barriers. Using visual tool boards, or shadow boards (Figure 1.3) is the key, and this approach has a positive impact on the productivity and floor space use in the work area. (The terms *tool board* and *shadow board* are used interchangeably; we will generally refer to them as tool boards.)

Placing tools on vertical boards eliminates the need for cabinets, shelves, and other horizontal storage and opens up floor space. Horizontal surfaces are needed only where work is performed. You would be shocked at the number of cases in which a workbench is used solely for storing tools and junk. After implementing 5S and the visual tools approach, the workbench can be removed from the area.

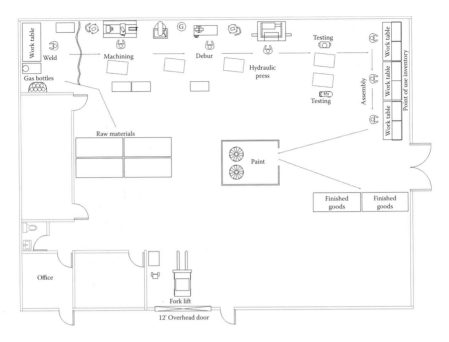

FIGURE 1.2
Visual layout.

Tool boards allow workers to quickly retrieve the exact item needed. They also show visually when the tool is missing or in use, creating an environment where tools are controlled and accounted for and the cost of replacing tools decreases.

VISUAL PARTS AND SUPPLIES

Parts and supplies are the next important consideration in a work area. The 5S philosophy is to create a specific location or home for every item in the factory and to provide clear marking, labeling, and designations. However, parts and supplies in a maintenance department, work area, assembly line, or any other place in the plant must also be managed through visual controls.

Applying 5S first makes sense. Sort through the parts and supplies not needed, and organize what is left. Then, mark off and label the storage area

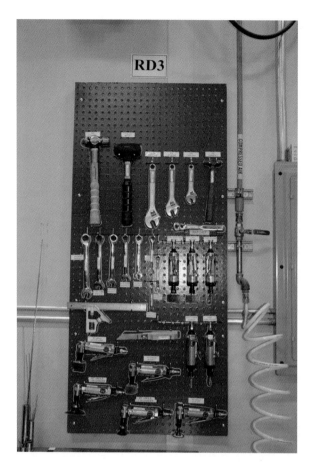

FIGURE 1.3
Tool board, or shadow board.

or tool board. These steps accomplish the 5S requirement. The next step is visual control.

When creating an environment for visual parts and supplies, you must develop a replenishment system that allows for the correct signals to trigger ordering. The visual control element here is critical. How much of the item should be on hand? What is the minimum quantity that will signal or trigger reordering? How much should be reordered? Who does it? Communicating that information visually is visual control.

Kanban, literally the Japanese word for "card" or "sign," is a Lean communication system for streamlining the process of ordering various parts, supplies, and material. Chapter 5 discusses the concept of kanban and key points for developing a visual system for the replenishment of parts and supplies. A visual control system for inventory will enable you to dramatically reduce cost and reduce the chance of running out of parts and supplies.

VISUAL MAINTENANCE AND TOTAL PRODUCTIVE MAINTENANCE BOARDS

A maintenance department represents a different environment and exhibits quite a different dynamic from an assembly line or work area. A multitude of tasks is performed, involving numerous employees, many tools and parts, special projects, and support tasks for the production floor. The need for a visually controlled environment is critical. Think of the downtown atmosphere of any big city. The amount of interaction going on simultaneously is mind-boggling, but it works through the use of visual controls that we often forget are even there. Designing a visual maintenance shop requires tremendous attention to detail, and Chapter 6 is dedicated solely to that environment.

When compared with an assembly workstation that has defined work and only the specific tools to perform that defined work, a maintenance department is a complex beast of parts, supplies, tools, equipment, and people. Tools alone create the first challenge, as each tool is used to perform more than one type of work. Maintenance team members need access to certain tools at certain times, and sometimes multiples of the same tool are needed. Community tool boards are essential to controlling tools and keeping costs down. Parts and supplies must also be organized and placed on a visual reordering system.

Most importantly, a standard visual total productive maintenance (TPM) system is needed to ensure that overall equipment effectiveness is achieved on the production floor. All machines or areas must have visual TPM boards displaying required maintenance work for both operators and maintenance staff. TPM boards act as a quick visual guide to keep those involved in TPM accountable for maintenance.

The maintenance department must also have visual schedules posting required TPM activities and special projects. This information is generally hidden in printed documents or on computers, when it needs to be on a board in the department similar to an arrival and departures board in airports. A visual maintenance department is an efficient maintenance department.

VISUAL COMMUNICATION

Visual communication is another element of a visual control system. Information on company performance must be made available to all employees on a visual communication board positioned at a place where people interact. Sales, profit, orders, quality, on-time delivery, and similar metrics must be accessible to all.

Workcells and departmental performance information (e.g., productivity, quality, safety, and output information specific to a given work area or team) must also be made visible in the respective areas. These boards act as a guideline for potential improvement ideas and goals. Visibility creates awareness, awareness creates action, action creates results, and results make customers and executives happy. Visual communication is covered in Chapter 7.

5S and the visual factory are, in our opinion, the most important elements of Lean manufacturing. You will find that, after "going visual," more and more opportunities to improve your factory will be exposed.

2

The Basics of the Visual Factory: 5S

To create a foundation for your company's visual factory, it is a good idea to start with a clear and concise understanding of the merits of 5S. A successful 5S implementation becomes the bedrock for a viable visual management system. Although closely related to each other, 5S and a visual management system are, in fact, two separate entities; the existence of the latter depends on a satisfactory implementation of the former. To assume they are the same is to suggest that simple mathematics and algebra are one and the same.

5S is focused on where items belong, on identifying a specific location for everything in the work area. A visual management system builds on 5S and is intimately tied to the production operation by directing the flow of work, summoning new parts from inventory, initiating and stopping production, and aiding the identification, correction, and disposition of products with quality problems.

THE 5S'S

This chapter provides a detailed explanation of the 5S methodology and how to implement a 5S system. We begin with an explanation of the 5S's, which you can also think of as five successive phases:

- Sort
- Set in order

- Shine or scrub
- Standardize
- Sustain

Sort

Sorting is the act of removing and discarding all unnecessary items from a given work area or, from a plant perspective, company-wide. It is usually best to start 5S implementation in a specific area to help keep focus. You would be surprised how difficult the sorting function can be. We humans love our "stuff" and struggle to part ways with even the most unnecessary and infrequently used possessions; witness the growth of the self-storage industry over the years. In a manufacturing environment, items can accumulate very quickly and create quite a mess, making everything less visible.

Anything can be removed, from major pieces of equipment down to paper clips and small pieces of hardware. This "detox" phase allows the implementation team to see what items are truly needed to conduct the work.

Set in Order

This second phase of 5S is the act of aggressive organization, from setting up the work area from the ground floor and identifying where workbenches and other items will be positioned all the way up to designing tool boards, labeling items, and designating and labeling locations for things—in a nutshell, creating a world where everything has a home.

In preparation for the set-in-order phase, you must stock up on supplies to help create the visual workplace, including the following:

- Colored floor tape
- Spray paint
- Label maker
- Laminating supplies
- Paint pens
- Tape measures
- Velcro tape or double-sided tape
- Red tags (explained in this chapter)

Shine or Scrub

While this phase of 5S is mostly self-explanatory, it is important. It involves thoroughly cleaning the entire area including tools, bins, shelves, equipment, and workbenches, to create a showroom condition. During this phase of 5S implementation you are attempting bring the area back to its original state and appearance—not its original layout but its original level of cleanliness.

Standardize

Standardize is defined differently among Lean practitioners. To keep it simple for this book, standardization in 5S means maintaining some level of consistency in the application of the visual workplace. First, develop an overall color-coding system for the facility by assigning a unique color to every different department and process, for example:

- Shipping—blue
- Fabrication—red
- Maintenance—green
- Assembly 1—black
- Assembly 2—orange
- Workcell 1—yellow

Next, assign colors to identify the location of items within work areas. These will be applied consistently throughout the plant and will be used mainly for floor items. For instance, yellow floor tape could signify items positioned behind workers. Green floor tape could be used to identify the location of garbage cans and recycling bins. Black floor tape could mean finished goods. Do whatever makes sense for your environment.

Sustain

In this fifth and final phase of a 5S implementation, checks and balances are put in place to maintain the area and to allow for further improvement. End-of-day clean-up procedures, auditing, tracking, and incentive programs can all be used. Techniques for sustaining 5S are covered in further detail in the section on 5S events that follows.

5S implementation is always a good starting point for a Lean journey. 5S is highly visible; it provides "tangible" results, whereas other elements of Lean implementation, such as a new changeover procedure or a total productive maintenance (TPM) program, are often harder to see.

LET THE 5S EVENT BEGIN

Kaizen events provide a good mechanism for implementing a 5S system. Kaizen events are simply a method of organizing Lean projects, involving a team of individuals who come together during a set time frame and improve an area by removing waste. A kaizen team can implement 5S in a work area in a very short time.

The end goal of any 5S team is to make an area "5S compliant" by the end of the kaizen event. Essentially, this means that every item required to perform the work—and only those items—has a home in the work area. Everything has a location, and the location and item are clearly marked. It is important to complete each "S" in order before moving on to the next, at least as best you can. Following is a typical agenda for a 5S implementation kaizen event.

5S Day 1: Sort

During the sorting phase, all items deemed unnecessary should be removed from the work area as well as any items that are "questionable." Questionable items are those not used often—that is, not everyday necessities. The team needs to decide on the home location for infrequently used items. The team leader should break the team into two subteams to begin the sorting portion of 5S:

- Sorting team
- Collection team

Sorting Team

The sorting team is responsible for sifting through the workstations and identifying all unnecessary tools, supplies, tables, chairs, garbage cans, and other equipment. It is best to use production workers on the sorting team. They have the detailed knowledge of the workstations and can help the other team members. Pair up a production worker with someone who does not work in the area. This allows for an outside eye to play "devil's advocate" and to question the use of items in the workstations.

Cabinets, drawers, and tool chests should be completely emptied out, and items should be sorted through to identify the essentials. Always start with the small items, which quite seriously includes extra pens, pencils, and wrenches. A collection of these small items can easily require medium-sized storage bins, organizers, shelves, and tables. Medium-sized items require large storage areas such as workbenches, cabinets, tool chests, and racks. Large items require floor space, and floor space requires buildings and facilities. See the point?

Remember, one of the main goals of a 5S team is to achieve more open floor space, to better use current floor space, and to reduce the waste of motion and transportation. Opening up existing floor space is essential to growth—to adding new products and product lines while avoiding additional construction to the facility and incurring more cost.

To conduct the sorting activities, the team should use what is called a red-tag campaign. A red-tag campaign is an organized approach to sorting that allows many people to be involved and also prevents items from being taken from the workstations. There are three parts to successful red-tag campaign:

- Red tags
- Red-tag area
- Red-tag removal procedure

Red Tags

Red tags are visual indicators—literally red tags or cards—that a kaizen team attaches to items deemed unnecessary to perform the work in the workstation. The sorting team places these tags on items that are to be removed and brought to a red-tag area for further evaluation (Figure 2.1).

During 5S implementation kaizen events, quick decisions must be made at the sorting phase, because the bulk of the work is to be done during the second phase, set in order. This can be an emotional time for team members; as mentioned previously, people become very attached to their work belongings. In a five-day event, the red tagging and sorting need to be completed by the end of Day 1 to ensure that the team will be able to continue on schedule with the project.

FIGURE 2.1
Red tag.

Anything can be removed during a red-tag campaign. The list can go on and on, including the following:

- Extra air tools
- Extra hand tools (e.g., wrenches, screwdrivers, socket sets)
- Workbenches
- Lights
- Fixtures
- Garbage cans
- Chairs
- Documentation
- Cabinets and shelving
- Parts and material

The sorting team places red tags on all items pulled from the workstations, fills out the appropriate information, and places the items in the red-tag area.

Red-Tag Area and Collection Team

The red-tag area is a temporary staging area for the items that have been removed by the sorting team. This area should be marked off with red tape and identified clearly by hanging a sign in the area.

The collection team is required to be in the red-tag area. At this point in the process, nothing has left the building, and it is too early to take that step. The collection team receives everything brought by the sorting team to the red-tag area and organizes things based on the information on the red tag.

The collection team should create an inventory list of the red-tag items so that the team as a whole can decide on each item's fate. The inventory list also provides insight on the amount of money tied up in, for example, unnecessary supplies, tools, and workbenches.

Sorting Wrap-Up

Most of the first day will be spent sorting, and the team should focus on completing that phase by day's end. During lunch, the team leader should get a progress update from each subteam and provide any support or direction needed, including shifting people's roles as needed. One of the critical attributes of a good kaizen team leader is the ability to evaluate progress and make sure the team members are working on the right items at the right time.

Ideally, by the end of Day 1, the team should be in a position to begin thinking about the next "S" in the 5S implementation. The second "S" is set in order, sometimes called *straighten*. One of the best preparations for the set-in-order phase is to completely clear out the work area so that the actual floor space is empty. This allows the team to see the available space and then to piece together the work area in a way that will use the floor space more effectively. This is a grand opportunity for the employees who work in the area and are on the team to set up the work area as they see fit. The team leader provides support to ensure that the team is considering reduction in motion, transportation, travel distance, and better use of floor space. Therefore, the best situation to be in after Day 1 is to have the workstations and work area completely sorted, the red-tag area organized, and the work area completely cleared in preparation for the beginning of Day 2, set in order.

Red-Tag Removal Procedure

After Day 1 is complete, the team leader or kaizen champion should begin putting together a removal procedure for the items in the red-tag area.

This procedure does not need to be completed immediately, but a couple of criteria need to be established.

- Deadline: How long do you want to hold onto your junk? Do not get into a vicious cycle of moving garbage from one place to another in the factory. Establish a deadline for removal, such as 30, 45, or 60 days. Some red-tag areas can be cleared out in just one week. It depends on the items and what kind of "bond" the company has with the items. If it is deemed unwanted, get rid of it.
- Removal options:
  - Auction off the items to employees, or simply give them away.
  - Organize a "garage" sale.
  - Donate items to local nonprofit organizations and colleges.
  - Bring items to a local recycling facility.
  - Send items to a sister plant.
- As a last resort, throw items into the garbage.

5S Day 2 and Day 3: Set in Order and Shine

Start by ensuring again that all sorting activities are complete so the team can see what remains to be organized. The set-in-order phase takes the longest and is often the most tedious work. The purpose of set in order is to organize the area so everything has a home, thereby improving the flow of incoming material, work in process, and finished goods. Most important is the need to reduce floor-space use and travel distance. It does not matter whether the area is an assembly line, a workcell with machines and equipment, a shipping department, or an area with any other function. You can apply everything explained here to set in order and promote the flow of work.

Always go into the second "S" with the mind-set of making everything visual and accessible. Opening floor space and work surfaces is the key to any 5S implementation. Always remember to "go vertical" and to use dead space, which is everywhere. Employees seem to think flat surfaces are needed to store and hold supplies and items. Often, workbenches and tables are brought into a work area just to hold things. With a little creativity, almost anything can be stored vertically on tool and supply boards. Avoid using cabinets, drawers, and shelving as much as possible.

Some things, such as delicate calibration devices, do need to be stored behind a cabinet door, but the problem with doors and drawers is that they hide things and unnecessary and misplaced items will accumulate very quickly. When organizing items that must sit on shelves, suggest that the team make cubby holes to maximize shelf space and help keep it organized. Oftentimes the space in between stacked shelves is wasted dead space. Maximize available space by using subshelving.

Position Floor Items

Before you can get into the fine detail work of set in order, begin with the floor items. Decide what surfaces will be needed in the workstations and what areas will be used for the actual work. Always evaluate the amount of space truly needed to perform the job at hand. The team should decide what the flow of material and parts will be, begin piecing together the process, and come up with a few layout designs to choose from.

Any items that will go on the floor should be the first items placed in the work area, including the following:

- Work surfaces: for example, workbenches, conveyors, and tables
- Garbage cans: be sure to identify the minimum number needed, but also to take into account point of use to reduce motion
- Locations for staging for incoming and outgoing material, parts, and products
- Miscellaneous items: vacuums, welding machines, specialty equipment and machines

Nothing is permanent at this point, so do not start marking the floor with specific designations yet; instead, try to make tentative decisions on placement of all floor items.

This portion of set in order may take part or the whole of Day 2.

Create an Addressing System

Once the floor items are positioned, it is time to create designations or "addresses" for them. Simply make an outline around each item on the floor with floor tape to identify its location. The best approach is to mark off the locations for those items that can move. The locations of items bolted to the floor or heavy workbenches that will not move do not need to be marked with floor tape, but everything else should be. Once taping is complete, create the address designations using a label-making machine, and position each label on the floor in front of each piece of equipment. Figure 2.2 shows an overhead view of a work area with floor areas identified; as you can see, items on the floor are clearly outlined.

The 5S team should place labels or stencils on the floor that specify a unique address for each location. The team may want to use spray paint and stencils to mark off floor locations in environments that are dirt prone or where welding, dust, oil, debris, and hazardous materials are used; laminated floor labels may not work well in such areas. It is also important to place address designations up high as well as on the floor so that the addresses can be seen from a distance.

In Figure 2.2, A1 and A2 are used as the addresses at which important work-related items needed in the workstation will be located. It matters not what will go there just yet but that you have a unique address for each location. Any item to be stored at location A1, whether it is a calculator, tool, or bin material, will be physically labeled "A1" to show the address at which it belongs.

If any item is not returned to its proper location, anyone noticing it can quickly find its home. "Addressing" items is an extremely powerful approach that saves time, reduces motion and confusion, and helps reduce the purchasing and replacement of tools and supplies. Figure 2.3 and Figure 2.4 further illustrate the actual implementation of an addressing system.

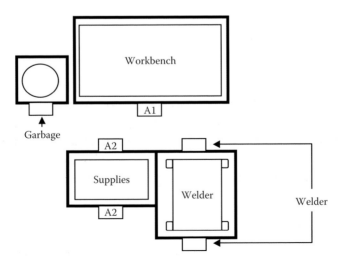

FIGURE 2.2
Floor identification.

FIGURE 2.3
Floor designations.

Organize Tools and Supplies

Once the team has decided on the locations of the floor items, take all the necessary tools, supplies, and various workstation-related items and lay them out in the workstation to see what needs to be organized. By starting the set-in-order phase with the mind-set of going vertical and avoiding flat surfaces, you challenge the team to come up with creative and innovative approaches to organizing. Bring in a cabinet, shelf, or tool chest only as an absolute last option. Remember, the key to 5S is visibility.

Tool Board Basics

Tools should be hung vertically on tool boards, or shadow boards, where they are visible and accessible. These boards are used to keep tools off work surfaces and allow operators to see them. We delve into the design and

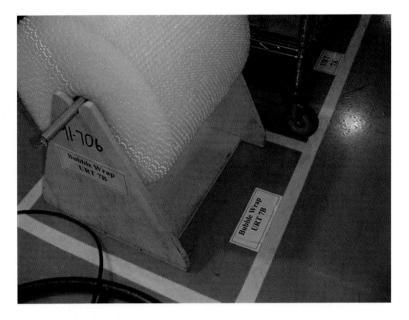

FIGURE 2.4
Floor markings

construction of tool boards in Chapter 4, but here are the basic steps and some tips to help you get creative with tool boards:

1. Paint the boards: Any color will work. The team leader should select team members to begin painting the boards (generally, pegboard is used) at the beginning of Day 2 so they will be dry for use when needed.
2. Tool layout: Once the boards are dry, lay them on the floor or another flat surface, and position all the tools and supplies on the board "cookie-cutter" style—tools, tape, scissors, calculators, clipboards, and whatever else will be used in the work area—to identify how large the board will need to be. Your kaizen supply box should contain pegs, double-sided tape, Velcro tape, and other supplies that can be used to hold things vertically.
3. Cut the pegboard to size: Now, remove the tools from the pegboard, and cut a square or rectangular piece sized appropriately for the workstation.
4. Install the tool board: Tool boards can be installed just about anywhere, as long as the location is accessible, is at the point of use, and does not disrupt the operator. They can be mounted on the wall,

attached to the side of a workbench or cabinet, and even placed on casters (wheels). If the tool board will be mounted on the wall, use a wooden frame of 1" x 1" studs to hold it. The pegs used to hang items need clearance behind the board to lock into place.

5. Hang the items: Now, the team members can hang and organize the tools and supplies on the tool board. Be sure to leave room for labels in between the items and space to draw a shadow or outline of each item. This process is relatively slow but is crucial to any 5S implementation. After placing the tools on the board, simply take the paint pens that should be in the event supply box and outline each tool on the board. This makes visible when a tool is being used or is missing. Next, make a name label for each item and place it near the item's location on the board.

6. The last step is to assign a designated address for each tool board (e.g., B5, J7, L3). This address must be listed physically on every tool, so that people know where it belongs. Figure 2.5 shows a good example of a tool board that was built using these six simple guidelines.

Shine and Scrub

As the area is organized, break out the kaizen event supply box, which should also include cleaning supplies. The set-in-order and scrub phases can be accomplished together. Always paint when possible to create a showroom appearance. Cleaning will get you only so far, but painting workbenches, shelves, metal stands, and so forth can make the area look new.

Clean and "shine" everything, eliminating all forms of contamination including dust, dirt, fluids, and other debris. Cleaning and shining tools and equipment can also help them operate better. Create a sense of workplace pride; the factory floor should be your showroom.

5S Day 4: Standardize

Day 4 is for fine-tuning and ensuring the team is completing tasks consistently. For instance, check that all tools are on pegboard and hung vertically, that the tool boards are painted to color code them, and that all tools are outlined and labeled appropriately. The tools on each board may be different, but the general appearance should be quite similar. Also, every item on the floor should be clearly marked with a location and identified with its name. Floor tape should be used consistently: yellow for caution,

FIGURE 2.5
Tool board example.

black for finished goods, red for items in the workstation, or whatever scheme the team has devised. Try to be standardized in your approach.

The team leader should now begin to create the report-out presentation that will be given to the company on Day 5 to outline the team's accomplishments. The presentation should include the following:

- Picture of the team
- List of team members' names and titles
- "Before" pictures of the areas involved
- Goals and objectives: for example, reduction in floor-space, travel distance, and motion
- "After" pictures
- Individual team member accomplishments
- Lessons learned
- Action item list: unfinished items to be completed within 30 days

5S Day 5: Beginning to Sustain

Try to schedule the report presentation at a time that will allow the most people to attend. The team leader should put the final touches on the presentation, and take any final pictures of the area to be used in the report. Team members can use this time to finish cleaning up the area, to finalize any labeling or other 5S items, and to put together an action item list of anything that did not get done.

The action item list is often called a 30-day mandate; it outlines what the unfinished task is, who is responsible, and when the deadline for completion is. Companies that struggle to see things through to completion can use this mandate as an opportunity to teach people how to follow through on tasks. Completing this list is vital to the success of the team and to those who will be working in the newly organized area.

After the presentation, the team should invite the attendees to tour the work area. A tour is a very good opportunity for people to see the tangible elements of Lean and to ask questions and give comments based on what they see. Explain the importance of the new 5S approach to organization and how it benefits everyone. Congratulate the team on their accomplishments, and then get some well-deserved rest.

5S IN MAINTENANCE DEPARTMENTS

Maintenance departments are perfect candidates for 5S implementations. Over time, maintenance commonly becomes the dumping ground for stuff, and maintenance personnel like to stock up for "what ifs." Often these "what ifs" never materialize, and unused items just build up. Maintenance departments also employ multiple people doing various repairs, preventive maintenance, and special projects. The maintenance department is a community work area, in which tools and supplies are shared. Sharing tools and supplies on an assembly line where there are definable workstations can be counterproductive—and even dangerous—by promoting wasted motion, the chance of losing tools, lost production, and reduced concentration. Work in these types of manufacturing processes is clearly outlined, and the workstations should have exactly what is needed to perform the work.

However, maintenance departments do not operate under these guidelines. Although there are defined preventive maintenance schedules for tasks to be performed regularly, there is also plenty of unscheduled work and special projects. Such work often requires that duplicate tools and supplies be available to be shared within the group. The creation of the inventory list on this type of 5S event is critical because many high-cost items may be eliminated. This type of environment is especially ripe for 5S.

5S should be implemented in a maintenance area through a scheduled kaizen event similar to one that would be done in an assembly line or other area of the production process. While 5S can be implemented outside of a kaizen event with a similar outcome, the implementation is slower.

TIPS FOR SUSTAINING 5S

As mentioned before, sustaining a 5S program is the hardest part. It is no different from trying to maintain any cultural change in an organization. Your sustaining efforts will never end; that includes continually improving on what was already implemented. Each company must find its own way with sustaining. Here are a few recommendations:

- Create an end-of-day clean-up procedure.
- Conduct a daily or per-shift walkthrough.
- Establish a 5S audit sheet.
- Create and maintain a 5S tracking sheet.
- Develop a 5S incentive program.

Create an End-of-Day Clean-Up Procedure

Put together a specific and detailed list of tasks that workers in a given area must complete roughly 15 minutes prior to leaving. Possible items to list include the following:

- Empty all garbage and recycle bins.
- Sweep the work area.
- Return all tools to their designated locations.
- Return all supplies to their designated locations.
- Place pallet jacks, garbage cans, chairs, and hand trucks in their designated locations.

Be sure to post the list and allow the operators time to conduct the clean-up.

Conduct a Daily or Shift Walkthrough

Each area supervisor should take a few minutes after everyone has left to walk through the work area and verify that the end-of-day clean-up was completed and that all items have been returned to home locations. If your company implements 5S at the detailed level described in this chapter, this supervisor walkthrough should be quick. Any small deviations from 5S can be quickly resolved during that walkthrough.

Establish a 5S Audit Sheet

You can also incorporate a weekly or monthly 5S audit. Develop a 5S audit sheet with information similar to the clean-up procedure (Figure 2.6).

Item 1 5S Audit Sheet

5S Audit Sheet

Work Area ______

Audit Date ______ **# of Yes's** ____ **/16 =** ____ **%**

Auditors ______

Sort (Get rid of unnecessary items)		
All non-production-related items have been removed	Yes	No
Excessive quantities of supplies and parts have been removed	Yes	No
Unnecessary equipment has been removed	Yes	No
Set in Order		
Tool boards are used and contain shadows, labels, and designations	Yes	No
All equipment and tools are clearly marked and well organized	Yes	No
Locations and containers for items, parts, and supplies are clearly marked	Yes	No
Material is setup on a kanban or two-bin system and is well organized	Yes	No
Scrub/Shine		
Floors, work surfaces, equipment, and storage areas are clean	Yes	No
Garbage and recyclables are collected and disposed of properly	Yes	No
Excess pallet and packaging materials are cleared out	Yes	No
Standardize		
Colors are consistent in each area and clearly defined	Yes	No
It is obvious through visual management whether tasks have been done	Yes	No
Sustain		
Audit scores are posted in each work area	Yes	No
Production control boards are being used on a daily basis	Yes	No
Work instructions are displayed with correct revision	Yes	No
Work area is clean, neat and orderly with no serious unsafe conditions observed	Yes	No

GREEN = 81% to 100% Area is 5S compliance

YELLOW = 66% to 80% Area meets minimal standards

RED = 0% to 65% Area needs immediate attention

FIGURE 2.6
5S audit sheet.

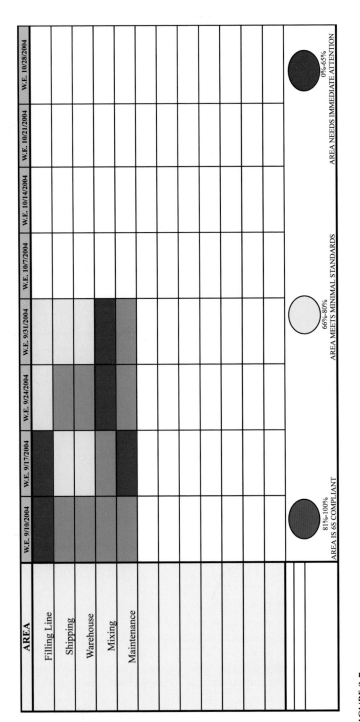

FIGURE 2.7
5S tracking sheet.

Create and Maintain a 5S Tracking Sheet

Display the scores from the 5S audits on a tracking sheet that is visible to the whole company. This creates awareness and healthy competition among the areas, and everyone can see how the plant is doing overall. The tracking sheet becomes a visual representation of the progress being made with 5S. Figure 2.7 is a simple example of a 5S tracking sheet, in which the colors green, yellow, and red denote the score levels good, needs improvement, and unacceptable, respectively.

Develop a 5S Incentive Program

The last suggestion is to develop an incentive program that rewards employees and work areas that prove to be champions of 5S. Hand out quarterly incentives such as gift cards, pizza parties, or bonuses to the area with highest 5S scores for the quarter. Areas not receiving this incentive will catch on fast and will begin to make more effort to sustain their areas and to improve what is already in place.

Once 5S is implemented throughout the factory, the foundation is set to support more advanced initiatives in your emerging visual management system.

3

Visual Factory Layout

This chapter explains how to make an overall assessment of your plant layout and turn it into a more productive visual factory. We also cover factors to consider for your new process layouts, including the importance of identifying work areas or work zones. These zones, explained in more detail later in the chapter, are used to visually show where the definable departments and processes are located. In all cases, each zone is located and laid out to promote the flow of work, including both production and support activities.

Let there be no question: the highest priority of any factory layout must be production processes—that is, the processes and people who make and add value to products. Everyone and everything else, no matter how critical in terms of providing key information or materials to manufacturing, is still a secondary priority when laying out a factory. Do you want support staff members placed near the production groups they support? The answer is most likely yes, with a caveat. We do want to encourage positive and productive human-to-human interaction and communication. What is needed most, however, is optimizing the flow of production processes while getting timely, accurate, and complete information into the hands of all those who need it, as they need it. When prioritizing placement within a new facility layout, production support functions, which exist primarily to serve manufacturing processes, are secondary to production processes.

THE LEGACY OF FACTORY LAYOUTS

Before we get into the nuts and bolts of visualizing and creating a visual factory layout, here are a few questions to think about.

- Have you ever wondered why your production facility is designed and laid out as it is? Are there aspects of the layout that defy logic, such as unnecessary product movement?
- Have you ever asked yourself why a piece of equipment is located and oriented in the plant as it is? For example, why is a particular machine located in the corner of a remote building, requiring products to be transported for processing via a complicated labyrinth?
- Does it seem as if there is no rhyme or reason to the layout of raw material in relation to the production line?

Following WWII, plant layouts in American manufacturing operations were often designed around the concept of consolidated operations, meaning that similar functions were colocated within the same vicinity—the welders in one area, the machinists in another, electrical assembly in yet another, and so on. The job of a scheduling and planning department was to ensure that each function was loaded up to a certain level of capacity. Plant layouts from that era also typically mirrored how the employees were organized into departments, with productivity measured and compensation paid in relation to the number of items produced by a given work area. The queues of products amassed between domains were seen as safety nets and often used as a visual indicator of how well the operation was performing. The bigger the stack of parts, the better they were doing.

Without the pressure of international competition, this production model was perceived as working quite well. In the front office, quoting systems factored in the time and costs of long setups and changeovers. The larger the batch size, conventional wisdom argued, the less the cost of the setup per part and, hence, the development of the economic order quantity (EOQ) formula. (EOQ remains a useful planning tool as long as it does not shift the focus from the critical importance of reducing and minimizing setup and changeover times.)

It was not until the threat of worldwide competition surfaced in the mid 1970s and began to hit the bottom line of U.S. producers that a painfully slow change began to occur. Conventional manufacturing wisdom was called into question. At a time when Toyota production system pioneers were hitting their stride with concepts and methods that would propel their company to the leading edge of global competitiveness, American manufacturers were still mostly committed to the old tried and true business model. The problem was that the old system of manufacturing was facing its mortality as the collection of concepts and methods now commonly recognized as *Lean manufacturing* evolved. A company that is not experiencing competition because the products it manufactures are unique can be an exception to the rule. However, even for those who have such a niche market, the benefits of increased margins that result when waste is removed from processes are still very positive. For everyone else, however, turning a blind eye to competition can lead to some very difficult decisions.

Why, then, do the ghosts of consolidated operations, stacks of works in progress (WIPs), and long setup times from days gone by still linger in North American factories? Good question. Remember, these new concepts and ideas started to trickle into the mind-set of American manufacturing executives and plant engineers only in the mid to late 1980s. Since then, many continuous improvement initiatives have failed, as the direct result of piecemeal, underfunded, and understaffed efforts. In fact, there are hints of ill-fated but oftentimes well-intended attempts to implement improvement concepts in nearly every production facility we visit. However, seldom are the proper foundations for success created—the building blocks that will support new activities and allow new ideas to flourish, including the necessary holistic training and plant layout changes.

Certainly, having a library of books on every popular business idea from the last few decades is no help if the books are not read and the teachings are not applied. But most failed improvement initiatives are a direct result of a change in company priorities—keeping alive the catch phrase "program of the month." More often than not, momentum dies because a senior executive is still deeply entrenched in conventional thinking and has not yet endured enough competitive pain to succumb to the dynamic and profitable reasons to get behind the initiative. Lesson learned: we are much better off when we are proactive with a good idea rather than being reactive.

Unless you have just designed and constructed a new facility, chances are you have inherited your building and equipment layout from a predecessor. And chances are neither the building nor the internal layout of equipment was designed with Lean concepts as the driving factor. If you did design your facility layout, chances are that changes in product mix or product configuration have rendered the original process design suboptimal. Although we do occasionally stumble upon a creative mind who designed a building around the concept of value-added processes, most often we find production processes fitted in and around building columns and separated between stacks of WIP and fire walls.

Odds are you are looking at a facility layout that could use a healthy dose of waste reduction and process improvement thinking—including a new process layout and the reinvention of how employees will interface mentally, physically, and visually with those processes. Enter the visual factory.

VISUALIZING YOUR VISUAL FACTORY

Picture how your production processes would look if they were designed with no wasted human motion, no wasted product movement, just enough incoming material to support what the process consumes, and a 100% first-pass quality rate. Perhaps the manufacturing area is marked as the "green" area within the facility. You can see signage and colors identifying the area and showing visitors and new employees the status of production activities. You might notice that the amount of incoming material balances with the rate of the production process. Kanban bins and cards, located at the point of use, communicate both what quantities of material should be there and when more parts are needed. Each part in the bin is oriented correctly for consumption to minimize wasted motion. Visual signals indicate to material handling when it is time to retrieve more parts and material—whether purchased or value-added items—and the exact location at which each item can be picked up.

Products with different configurations are being assembled and are flowing freely from one value-added operation to the next, with no more travel distance than necessary, and the "all-systems-go" operational status is indicated by a green andon indicator light. All finished goods are moving into the packaging area and are wrapped, labeled, and loaded for shipment without stopping.

You can see by the posted workmanship certification sheets that all production workers have been trained. Employees are focused and engaged in their value-adding activities, ensuring product compliance to specifications yet wasting no motion as they complete their work and usher it on to the next process step. Pareto charts show the past day's and week's quality reports and what actions were taken to prevent a recurrence of the one nonconformity that occurred. Easy-to-follow, up-to-date work instructions are on each computer screen (and they are actually controlled documents in the company's formal document control system). In fact, work instructions are provided in more than one language to suit the needs of the workers for whom English is a second language.

Now that you have visualized this ideal end state, create a sketch of what your new waste-free process might look like. Chances are you will see a very different and far more productive work area, with workers wasting little time and motion and totally engaged in their work, no build-up of work-in-process queues, some opened-up floor space, and a smile on the supervisor's face. In fact, as you include the resident experts (i.e., the production workers) in conceptualizing the new layout, you might find a bucketful of good ideas to make product flow even better.

Actualizing Your Visual Factory

Is your rough visualization even possible? Why not? Can your visualization become 100% reality? Maybe, maybe not, yet the *systematic* application of *systematic* improvement initiatives might get you closer than you think. Some people will resist the idea because it represents a significant change from the "tried and true." One approach to overcoming resistance is to involve these very people in creating the new layout based on a common understanding of a goal that has been set. Laying out a production facility normally does take time, analysis, effort, and enough data to quantify key elements. In other words, do not plan on getting there overnight. More than anything, it takes a team effort to find the optimal layout. Implementing a visual management system can be an uncomplicated effort once you have a well-conceived plant and process layout in hand.

General Guidelines

Across the board, there are some general guidelines to follow when creating a new or modified factory layout. The first step, as described in Chapter 2, is to complete a comprehensive set of 5S events. This will help free up floor space and organize all critical elements in support of the production operation.

As part of the visual management system, we also recommend color coding to distinguish each major work zone and then using each work zone's color to identify the workbenches, tools, and totes associated with that area. The assigned color will help as you prepare for the more detailed work of organizing each zone. Various floor marking symbols can be used to indicate aisles, work zones, work flow, electrical panels, parts bin locations, staging areas, and safety zones and to emphasize environmental issues. Andon lights, signage, and placards are often placed at higher levels. In between the two, at eye level, are general communication boards and process control and product quality information. Walls, if required, are also excellent candidates for the color schemes and for posting dynamic process control information, such as production and total productive maintenance (TPM) boards.

Conventional wisdom may suggest creating a factory-wide layout prior to conducting any 5S events. As Lean practitioners, we have found that this approach, albeit desirable, is seldom practical for plants producing a variety of product configurations or introducing new products. Budgetary and capacity constraints often dictate the decision to focus on one area at a time within the facility.

Addressing Waste when Planning the Visual Factory

Systematically finding and minimizing (or completely removing) waste occurs during 5S events and also as you scrutinize each process that is a candidate for a new layout. For the purposes of this chapter, we will discuss seven of the eight Lean wastes, which were outlined in the introduction.

Overproduction

Whenever we produce (or buy) more materials and products than are needed to meet customer demand, we are falling back into the old production model of bygone days. Although still a common waste in American manufacturing, many operations managers are beginning to grasp the merits not just of avoiding overproduction, especially between work areas, but also for finished products. Many manufacturing managers now understand the increased costs and risks of producing more than what is needed, including unnecessary floor space, obsolescence, damaged products or materials, and lost opportunities.

> Overproduction bottom line: Produce only what is needed to complete the customer's order.

Waiting

Waiting is an unplanned stoppage of value-adding activities and is a huge waste of time and money. Productivity is minimized or shut down completely while an employee, machine, assembly line, or workcell waits for something needed to resume production. The holdup can be lack of information, such as decisions pending from a meeting, a quality assurance (QA) disposition decision, data required from a customer, or the latest engineering change order; missing parts or raw material; a machine cycle that needs to be completed; or a coworker who has not returned from a break. No matter what the cause, employees and capital equipment are idle but are still being paid for. Understanding the root causes of waiting and then systematically removing those root causes will provide financial dividends.

> Waiting bottom line: Waiting is costly; identify the causes and eliminate them.

Motion

Processes requiring human involvement may also require a certain amount of motion. For the purposes of process layout, a 5-foot diameter is appropriate for a work area where human motion is expected. Any required movement outside that work area is considered excessive and should be questioned. Reaching out, up, and down are also red flags; look for ways to avoid these movements to minimize the wear and tear on workers. Looking, bending, or reaching for tools or information, walking to get tools, parts, or approvals, or any other motion outside the work area needs to be scrutinized closely. When human motion is minimized or eliminated with a few simple changes in the process layout, the associated wasted time and wear and tear on the employees are eliminated as well.

> Motion bottom line: Design processes in a way that allows employees to complete their work without excessive motion. Avoid injuries to employees by keeping items safely close at hand.

Overprocessing

Anytime we handle a part unnecessarily or try to add features that exceed specifications, we are overprocessing. More often than not, a specification is fuzzy and leaves too much room for interpretation. An obvious example is the surface finish expected from a grinding, sanding, or polishing process, but there are others. In these cases, the assessment of whether a specification has been met is often subjective, and no two people will share the same opinion. Overinspection is also a form of overprocessing—by spending too much time trying to determine if a part conforms to specification or trying to find a defect that is not there. In both cases, the result is wasted time and effort.

> Overprocessing bottom line: Spending time creating an unnecessary value-added feature or overinspecting adds only unnecessary time and cost to a product, not additional value for the customer.

Transportation

We see it all the time—a product traveling more than absolutely necessary as it moves between value-added processes. Product travel presents a twofold opportunity.

First is the opportunity to reduce the actual distance a part travels throughout its journey on the manufacturing floor. We want to move the product the minimum distance necessary to accommodate machine work areas or human work zones. The physical size of some large fabrications, or even the internal work envelope of some machines, may make the goal of zero extra travel distance difficult to achieve. For the purposes of this book, we will consider the distance required to get a part to the machine, and not the movement within a machine's work zone, as product travel. (That said, optimized programming for computed numerically controlled [CNC] machines is seldom realized inside the work envelope. We will not delve into CNC programming opportunities in this book, but note that eliminating wasted movement in a CNC machine, and thereby minimizing machine cycle times, is a great improvement opportunity.)

The second major opportunity in the transportation category involves the orientation of a part or product as it is moved through the factory. The initial time and effort to orient a part to a known point of reference (or datum) is certainly not free. Yet we often observe a part being removed from a machine or assembly line, in a way that disrupts its proper orientation. That same part will require more processing downstream, and it will have to be reoriented. In an ideal world, once an item's orientation is established, that orientation is maintained until the completed product is received by the customer. For that matter, why not specify incoming products to be oriented a certain way on receipt from a supplier—so they are ready to go at their first setup? Any additional product travel or reorientation is simply waste.

Transportation bottom line: Move the part only the minimum distance required from one value-added operation to the next, and, once a datum is established for a part, maintain the part's orientation until all work is completed.

Excess Inventory

A certain level of inventory is required to maintain an ongoing flow that meets customer demand. However, care must be taken not to buy and carry more inventory than is necessary. In the purchased part inventory area, aim for proper levels to sustain your business. Given the increasing reluctance of worldwide suppliers to inventory raw material and components, keeping inventory levels down can be a matter of the strength and trust of your company's relationships. However, you have more control over your own shop floor by keeping WIP levels in balance with value-added activities. Any additional WIP is tying up cash.

> Excess inventory bottom line: Drive WIP inventory levels down to balance with the pace of value-added activities.

Rejects and Scrap

It goes almost without saying that any process that is creating rejects or scrapped parts is wasting material, process time, and the time of production and support personnel dealing with nonconforming product and discussing its disposition. Some factories build "rework lines" to salvage value from nonconforming product. Others simply devalue product to a "B" grade and accept reduced margins. The cost of a nonconforming product reaches far beyond the original cost of making the item. A properly implemented formal quality system, inclusive of training on and use of applicable process control methods and techniques, provides a huge step toward reducing the frequency of rejected and scrapped product.

> Reject and scrap bottom line: Spend the time and money to create processes that are capable of making products in compliance with specification the first time through.

After these seven wastes are removed as much as possible, we can look at the value stream of the preeminent products, based on a combination of dollar value, product volume, and product size. For larger parts and products, consideration for overhead cranes, track systems, and other transportation machinery becomes a primary factor in creating a new process, with a major impact on layout creation. Even though we must strike a balance among the many factors involved in a facility layout, some products are higher priority and should be considered first. All layout decisions should support the reason a manufacturing company is in business: to create value and in return make money.

OVERALL SEQUENCE FOR CREATING A VISUAL FACTORY LAYOUT

When designing a factory layout, start with the smallest amount of floor space required to accommodate the minimum sequential steps of the production value-adding steps (the attributes your customer is willing to pay for). The primary layout goal is to get the highest priority product from start to finish in the shortest time possible, leaving no queues between process steps, no wasted transportation, and no wasted human motion. That process should be visually indicated in the factory by outlining it with colored tape or paint on the floor and creating signage that provides critical information.

Then, in concert with the value-added processes, determine production capacity needs, and calculate the correct usage rates and inventory levels for the materials, parts, and subassemblies required to sustain the desired rate of production. Once a satisfactory layout accommodates these two core components of the production matrix, and only then, are the space requirements of direct support groups (maintenance, quality assurance, planning, and supervisory personnel) that directly interact with the production processes considered.

Finally, consider the area requirements for indirect support personnel typically considered to work in overhead functions (e.g., sales, plant management, engineering, materials, product development, finance, safety, environmental). As you determine final layout options, also begin settling in on how to use a visual communication system to augment the existing communication processes.

THE FOUR BASIC CONDITIONS OF VALUE-ADDING PROCESSES

Value-adding processes, whether highly specialized or quite standard, are the operations through which the company adds value to an item and ultimately makes its money when it is sold and shipped to its final destination as a completed subassembly, final assembly, machined part, fabricated structure, or molded part. Four basic activities or conditions exist in value-added processing, and in only one is value actually being added.

The four basic manufacturing process activities or conditions are as follows:

- Value is being added to an item.
- The process is being reconfigured (at setup or changeover) to run a new product configuration.
- Planned stoppage (i.e., preventive maintenance [PM], plant shutdown).
- Unplanned stoppage (process or quality problem, outage).

From a visual management system standpoint, we want to know and communicate the general status of the process, as it occurs, to all those who will benefit, by using operational visual controls. Let's start by taking a look at these four basic conditions and some essential considerations for establishing a system of visual controls to communicate them.

Value Is Being Added

This condition justifies the use of a green indicator light to signify that all systems are "go." Why do we need to communicate this? A green light should mean not only that the process is running but also that it is "in control." Incorporating process control information will also show when the process is operating within specification but is out of control and trending toward going out of compliance. We want to know about an unfavorable trend before it becomes an actual problem. Therefore, it is as important to know when the process is working properly as to know when there is something wrong. Here are some things to consider visually communicating during normal value-adding processing:

- Customer demand (work order or sales order number, total quantity, due date)
- Performance to takt time (units/time period)
- Current work order fulfillment status (percentage completed)
- Visual indicators of line or machine status (green/yellow/red)
- Two-bin system (material replenishment)
- Status of defective or scrapped units
- Status of waste stream ("A" grade vs. "B" grade by-products; e.g., the runner system from a plastic injection molding process sent to the regrind operation; grade "A" represents a higher purity in the regrind material compared with grade "B" which has a higher level of impurities)
- Status of coolant system (particulate count in cutting fluid being recycled)
- Movement of heavy items (use of overhead crane, forklift)
- Transport of products from one process to another

Process Is Being Reconfigured (Setup or Changeover)

Even though setup and changeover (we will use these terms interchangeably) occur in value-adding processes, the process is not adding any value when it is being reconfigured. When a production operation is down for any reason, including setup or changeover, we want to know and visually communicate that information. Setups and changeovers must be planned, organized, resourced, and safely completed in the fastest possible time. Here are some guidelines for what information to communicate and what indicators to use:

- Process is not adding value: A simple red indicator light can be used to show when the value-added process is down.
- Status of setup or changeover metric: Think of this as the status bar in a dialog box on your computer when you are loading software. Setup, like a software download, has two main metrics: percent complete and rate. An entire setup, in terms of required steps and total time, is represented with a 100% bar, just as when loading software. As progress is made toward completing the setup or changeover, the status "bar" reflects the percent of completion. The rate, or speed of the setup, is a measure of how fast we complete the setup. Since time really is money for setups, an organized triage approach (all available hands on deck)

can help reduce downtime. Items that may make sense to measure for each setup are as follows:
- Planned start time
- Actual start time
- Planned duration (broken down by specific steps)
- Actual duration (by step).

Another tool to use for a setup or changeover is a countdown timer. This idea is already in use for airline travel. Next time you walk down the jetway, see if you can find the timer. It is visible to gate agents, flight attendants, and pilots and communicates how much time remains until the aircraft door should be closed, leading to the plane being pushed back from the gate. In production environments, this visual management tool is used to report the status of all four previously mentioned value-added elements and encourages others to help out.

Visual reporting of a setup or changeover could be as simple as showing which of these four primary steps is taking place:

1. Preparation: Even before a machine or production line has stopped running the last item, external setup steps for the next configuration should be under way. In fact, it is best to plan when the setup will start and when it will end. Visual tools provide both a communication mechanism and an accountability aid.
2. Mounting or removing parts or fixtures: Normally there is no way around stopping a process when it comes to mounting or removing parts and fixtures. The question is how fast it can be done safely while ensuring quality. If an anomaly occurs when changing hardware, we want to communicate that and immediately get the help needed to resolve the situation.
3. Measurements: During the measurement step, the setup team verifies that all elements—programs, tools, probes, parts, conveyors, fixtures, and operators—are working in harmony to produce compliant products before production can commence. If robust setup standards have been established ahead of time, this step may be fast. However, many operations are in trial-and-error mode when measuring a setup, which can be a protracted and time-consuming process. Therefore, it is critical to monitor and report how the measurement phase is going.

4. Trial runs: A well-thought-out process control procedure can help minimize trial runs required to verify that product is within specification. Actually, companies should find ways to remove the variables that drive the need for trial runs at all. In the meantime, establish a means to keep the number of trial runs to a minimum—and if trial parts must be made, ensure that they entail a minimum of wasted time and effort.

Planned Stoppage

Stoppages are seldom a good thing, but it is easier to accommodate the impact of a stoppage when it is planned. Good communication can minimize the negative impact of a planned stoppage. Whether it is a plant shutdown with a planned time for restart or simply a scheduled preventive maintenance activity for a machine, visually communicating the information to everyone eliminates confusion and improves an understanding of who will be impacted, what resources may be needed, and where they will be needed.

Unplanned Stoppage

These are the stoppages that can cause deep pain for production and for the company's pocketbook; they must be avoided at all costs. When they do occur, clear and comprehensive visual communication of expectations for how employees should respond is critical. Examples of unplanned stoppages include the following:

- A machine breaks down.
- A product is found to be nonconforming to specification.
- A process is found to be trending out of control.
- A problem is detected with a tool or fixture.
- The setup or changeover time is becoming excessive.
- A problem just occurred with a supplied product.
- An employee just created an error.
- Absenteeism—one or more employees did not show up for the start of a shift.
- A safety accident or incident just happened.
- Environmental concerns—a major spill just happened.
- The labor–management dispute has just boiled over.

- An unexpected third-party compliance auditor is in the front lobby.
- Mother Nature just unleashed its fury (e.g., loss of power, flooding, high winds, ice, snow).

Although not all unplanned work stoppages are created equal, all do require action and effort to overcome. The typical unplanned stoppage is attributable to a quality problem, with the root cause often found in a product supplied from an upstream process, whether the supplier is internal or external.

Companies should prepare for such calamities before they occur. Plans can be communicated via training and supported with visual aids, such as a simple evacuation plan in the case of an emergency. Anything behind an unplanned stoppage—troublesome designs, processes, vendors—can and should be communicated visually.

VISUAL INVENTORY

Now, let's move on and cover the considerations for handling inventory in a visual factory.

Feed Materials and Consumables

On the production floor, a two-bin system for handling the replenishment of feed parts works well in many areas. Using colored kanban cards can enhance the replenishment cycle. Each of the two bins provides a temporary storage location for identical parts near the point of consumption. The number of parts in each bin is calculated based on consumption volume. Parts are pulled from one bin at a time. When the first bin becomes empty, it is a visible trigger to order another bin's worth of parts from inventory.

Nothing can shut down cash flow faster than a problem with material, whether the specific problem is a late delivery, short shipment of parts, defective parts, a recent engineering change, or simply receiving the wrong part. If there is a problem with a supplied product, it is important not to jump immediately to blaming the materials manager but to investigate root causes. It is absolutely critical to know that all the material entering your facility is, in fact, the correct material for consumption. That means that every bit of it is in complete compliance with the engineering specification it was purchased against. To that end, vendor performance should be communicated visually.

Visually reporting the performance of a vendor or supplier will accomplish three things:

1. It will show the supplier's salesperson that you are communicating to the world the salesperson's company's ability to hit pricing, delivery, and quality expectations.
2. It will show the supplier's competitors when they may have an opportunity to do more business with your company.
3. It will communicate to the supplier how you classify it and which strategy (and how much effort) it must employ to work successfully with your company.

Purchased Inventory

In the stockroom, no part, subassembly, or raw material should ever be entered into inventory until it is known to be a compliant part to specification and is identified as such. Visually indicate stock levels and reorder points in the purchased part inventory locations.

WIP

The most accurate visual management tool for WIP is to see no WIP, except for parts that are actually having valued added to them. If that is not what one sees, a plan of action to get there should follow.

Finished Goods

The finished goods location, if your company has one, can be in proximity to the manufacturing area but should be segregated from the production processes. The finished goods area should be designed to accommodate the company's strategic inventory levels for various product configurations and identified as such. Visual controls can indicate where and how many finished goods are to be stored.

Another factor to consider for all inventory layouts is to provide for a first-in, first-out (FIFO) flow of material. Maintaining only required levels of inventory at each inventory stage and identifying and shedding unnecessary inventory will make it easier to achieve a working FIFO inventory system.

LAYING OUT SUPPORT FUNCTIONS

We have discussed some high-level factors to consider for the layout of value-adding processes and have explored which visual management tools we can apply. We have also discussed some visual management methods for incoming materials as well as for finished goods inventory. Now, let's take a look at issues to consider when laying out the functions that support the production and inventory processes.

Common Area

Start with the common area, which supports the critical "human" element for your employees. This area should be designed to accommodate employee breaks, lunch, and short standup meetings and should be adequately accessible from the production floor. It is also a great place to use as the hub for reporting key components of your visual management system. Make it a pleasant place to destress before folks go back to work. We recommend that you locate the restrooms very close to but not in the common area—perhaps just around the corner or down the hall. (Depending on the size of the facility, of course, you may also need additional restrooms in other locations.)

Direct Support Functions

Next on the list of priorities are the direct support functions for the production operation.

Supervisory Personnel

If your company is structured with production supervisors or team leaders, these folks belong as close to the production area as possible, preferably right in their area of responsibility. These are the unsung heroes who embrace one of the most difficult jobs in the company: ensuring the synchronization of employees and processes to meet production delivery commitments, all the while enforcing compliance with company policies and government regulations.

Maintenance

In equipment-intensive environments especially, make provisions for maintenance resources to provide timely and adequate technical support. It is not necessary to locate all maintenance department personnel and tools in one area. However, it is a good idea to allow for a common maintenance area as a safe place to fabricate, saw, and otherwise locate large or expensive tools, machine calibration equipment, and diagnostic equipment.

Whatever your exact layout, a visual chart showing the status of all machines and processes supported by the maintenance team should be proudly displayed and updated with each shift. A TPM program will report the preventive and corrective activities that are under way at any given time. A TPM board (described in more detail in Chapter 6) is a good way to visually communicate the status of the production capacities.

Tooling

As with inventory locations, tooling support should be in proximity to the machines being supported. All tooling (or cutters) should be sharpened and set in tool holders ready for use. One use of visual controls for tooling is to visually communicate parts readiness for the next work order by way of an organized and labeled tooling cart.

QA

Manufacturing leaders that demonstrate best-in-class attributes embrace quality in different ways. One thing they all have in common is a formal quality system that organizes and documents how the enterprise will provide quality products to its customers. Employees are fully trained to understand and operate within the scope and culture of the quality system. Whether the question is how to select a correct document revision or which workmanship standard may apply in a given situation, a company-wide approach to ensuring product quality is key to the global supply of quality products and services.

The quality control (QC) aspect of QA typically fulfills two roles. The first is to ensure that incoming products are in compliance with engineering specifications. Oftentimes this is called incoming inspection or, if the activity takes place at the supplier's site, source inspection. The second role QC fulfills is the in-process verification of product compliance with specification. Ideally, the machine operator or line assembler is able to use process control methods to ensure product quality themselves, and QC personnel are required only to review documentation. Regardless, a location for product verification must be specified, and visual controls are required. The use of special measurement instrumentation may require establishing a "clean-room" environment, if such equipment cannot be integrated into the production process. Place the instrumentation room close to the operation it supports. Inspection reports, first-pass rate numbers, defects with causal codes, and corrective action reports are all opportunities to visually communicate the quality status of the process.

Another space consideration for the quality function is identifying a securable location to accommodate nonconforming product that is awaiting disposition. This area needs to be established to prevent the unintended reintroduction of nonconforming product back into production. For some contracts involving government-supplied material (GSM) or special customer-supplied material, a separate and secure location may also be required in the layout.

Planning

Planning personnel play a huge role in how seamlessly a manufacturing area operates. Creating a good production plan starts with understanding work area capabilities and capacities and company strategies for loading work. Visually showing capacities, planned and actual loading goals, and planned and actual completion dates for each work center is paramount in communicating the larger production plan.

The planning function does not need to be located on the production floor, but the closer the better. The key consideration in the planning–production relationship is that the two-way flow of timely information never ceases. It is the ultimate closed-loop information system, constantly checking actual performance to the plan. In companies where the plan is a moving target, it may be time to rethink how a more stable plan can be obtained.

A semiaccurate master production schedule (MPS) (rarely is an MPS completely accurate) can go a long way toward shoring up production's chances of hitting delivery expectations. Post the MPS for all to see. When edits are made, repost the MPS.

When planning does face problems with feed parts, visually show the parts and what proactive action is under way to resolve the short-term situation and to prevent it from happening again. Last but not least, visually communicate the plan.

Indirect Support Functions

Finally, consider the positioning of the indirect support functions.

Materials Supply

There are two roles in the typical materials function. The first role, procuring material and having it ready for consumption, often falls under purchasing. Since purchasing agents and buyers must work closely with engineering specifications, they should be as close to engineering as they are to manufacturing.

The second role is ensuring the timely delivery of materials, in the correct quantity and at the right time, to the point of use. The key here is defining the manner in which feed material and parts (inventory) are stocked and how each part or item will be delivered to the point of use in the factory. Oftentimes the people in this role are referred to as parts handlers. They are essential in ensuring that unplanned production stoppages are avoided.

Some companies make the mistake of having production personnel stop what they are doing to retrieve the parts they need for their work. Assigning parts handlers or developing some type of automatic replenishment system to deliver the correct amount of product to the production line is a better method. A simple kanban system works wonders for most production operations.

Manufacturing Engineering

Whether your plant employs manufacturing engineers, industrial engineers, or process engineers, all engineers need equal access to plant management, product engineering, and manufacturing processes. No matter how they are defined, these roles support existing production processes—and normally support new product implementation and new processes as well.

Manufacturing engineers, working in tandem with shop-floor supervisors, are tasked with creating operational visual controls that show the real-time status of a process's performance. Depending on the level of interaction required and the need for process control, manufacturing engineers may need a place to work right in the heart of the production area. If a less intensive relationship is required, they can be located slightly away from the factory floor. Visual management opportunities may include such items as the efficiency of the process design, product takt times, cycle times, and analytical quality and product data reporting.

Production Management

Unlike the intimate daily involvement of team leaders and shop-floor supervisors with production operations, production management personnel create the operational tactics to successfully implement company strategic goals. Therefore, in terms of the visual management system, the tactical visual controls of production management provide a holistic view of the combined performance of processes, products, and people. Their offices may be away from the production floor—but not too far since they will need to verify the current state frequently and to have confidential conversations with plant personnel.

Product Engineering

Some factories have no product engineering activities on site. However, how a product's features are specified plays a huge role in dictating the cost of producing it. Specifications for material selection alone can dictate as much as 70% of the cost of making a product. A product's manufacturability is also a primary determining factor of its cost (e.g., whether it requires an unnecessary expensive machine versus an inexpensive one).

Product designs can be measured for their ease (or difficulty) to produce. Therefore, even though product engineers do not need to be located near the production floor, they should be close enough to observe how the product they designed is performing in manufacturing.

Safety and Environmental Functions

In any factory, accidents can result in staggering costs, resulting not only from liability and insurance claims but also from the loss of a valuable worker. Most states have safety reporting requirements, which are conducive to visual reporting. However, a safe work environment starts with the positive attitude of each and every employee toward safe work habits. Use your visual management system to reinforce safe working habits.

When laying out a factory, safety considerations are many. Placement of the safety manager's office is of secondary consideration compared with where a first aid or nurse's station is located. The first aid or nurse's stations must be located on or very near production activities where data show accidents and incidents are most likely to occur. Unless the safety manager's office is the first aid office, it can be at a more distant location.

Of course, you should check local code to ensure compliance with regulations. Ensure that provisions are made for all safety items, including a safety or first aid room as well as egress considerations. One such example is the floor marking around a wall electrical panel. Mark the floor with paint as a visual control to keep that area clear. Another example is the correct use of a lock-out–tag-out system. The tagged machine is down, and that information is visually communicated to all. Back at the breaker panel, the breaker should be prevented from being moved to the power position through the lock-out feature, which can also communicate who locked out the machine. When an area is under construction or otherwise needs to be secured, cones and safety tape are visual means of keeping people safe.

If you are located in the United States, your facility is subject to federal and state (and perhaps even local) environmental codes and regulations. Problems with emissions, spills, or other environmental dangers must be reported, and the steps to achieve compliance should be outlined. The visual management system provides a good means for communicating the steps taken by the company to comply with such regulations and what steps employees must take when faced with such an event.

Finance

Companies have different policies on how much and what financial information is shared with employees. However, when pertinent financial information is shared based on the whole company's performance, the common message is we need to work as a team. In the visual factory, this should go a step further: to generate better buy-in and ability to execute company strategies. Ideally, finance should communicate with each functional group what is needed (in terms of actual performance) with an understanding of how they, as a team, can help make the numbers more favorable.

Posting financial information may be a touchy issue, especially in privately held companies, but there are ways to share critical financial numbers while protecting information not deemed appropriate to share publicly. With proper encouragement, financial staff can be very creative in finding a happy medium that achieves the benefits that come from employee participation.

The financial staff members typically do not need to be located close to the factory floor. However, for those involved in establishing budgets and creating standard costing, it helps to have regular access to the manufacturing managers and manufacturing engineering managers.

Plant Management

In a visual factory, plant management personnel are often the individuals tasked to coin the visual management strategy and therefore the associated visual controls. These are the high-level visuals that communicate culture, mission, and corporate direction. Although these individuals do not need to be located right next to production, they do need to make frequent contact with all factory personnel to reinforce the strategies. In addition, the powerful benefits that result from senior managers showing an interest in people and processes throughout the factory cannot be achieved in any other way.

Sales

The sales function represents the cornerstone of most manufacturing businesses. The role of sales is to sell value-added products to customers—and then to successfully communicate to the rest of the organization what customers want. This activity must include accurately capturing sales order information that reflects what products customers actually need and what they expect for after-sales service.

A common disconnect occurs when sales or customer service personnel do not understand the impact of an incorrectly entered sales order. Yet, as the old saying goes, junk in, junk out. A miscue on the part of sales can drive a costly sequence of undesirable events that can include manufacturing the wrong product configuration, the resulting rework, and late delivery. A visual report showing the accuracy of sales orders in capturing what was wanted by the customer can go a long way to ensure timely deliveries. Visually communicating what a customer wants is an even better way to avoid expensive blunders. The best example may be a sample part—exhibiting all desired physical attributes and operational features. Oftentimes a written specification, engineering sketches, or drawings help remove all doubt as to what is actually wanted.

Office Support Personnel

Customer service, information technology, receptionists, and other office support personnel normally do not need to be very close to production. However, the closer together they work, the greater the sense they will have of being part of the same team.

Overall Support Services

In creating a factory layout, provisions must be made to accommodate all support services and equipment, including utilities, communication systems, computer networks, paging, and telephone systems. With the ongoing emergence of digital technology, consider providing room to accommodate state-of-the-art developments.

BACK TO YOUR FUTURE FACTORY LAYOUT

Let's revisit your visualization of your new plant layout. Make a list of hurdles to overcome in achieving your productive visual factory. Systematically eliminate or secure each roadblock as you work toward settling on a final solution. When you get buy-in from the team and support from plant management, enjoy implementing a waste-free layout, with the full complement of your new visual management system.

Last but not least, picture yourself giving a guided tour of your facility to a group of visitors. What do you want them to see? (Keep in mind that there may be some areas considered off limits due to the proprietary nature of the work being done.) After giving adequate consideration to your new layout, complete the effort by adding the route for a standard factory tour, complete with painted aisles and other visual guides along the way.

Now, step back and take a few minutes to enjoy your new visual factory layout. At the same time, realize that your new creation will need to change as new and different business drivers will surface tomorrow, next week or next month.

4

Visual Tools

In Chapter 2, we introduced the construction of visual tool boards or shadow boards. This chapter on visual tools reviews the basics and explains how to design and create tool boards or shadow boards in greater detail. Designing and constructing tool boards can be tough, and companies implementing 5S often struggle with this element of the visual factory. There should be no confusion after reading this chapter.

We will then get into the concept of right-sizing: the Lean concept of presenting tools and parts in a way that reduces the amount of money one spends on the storage of useless items. In this case, we are talking about designing the presentation of tools and parts in a customized fashion to reduce space and travel distances.

As you know by now, 5S is a philosophy of aggressive organization and cleanliness that creates order and discipline and lays the groundwork for a visual factory. As you may recall, the benefits of 5S include the following:

- Reduced production cycle time
- Reduced downtime
- Safer environment
- Increased available floor space
- Reduced waste of motion and overproduction
- Creation of a visually pleasing shop
- Visibility of potential issues

Organizing tools visually fall under the second phase of the 5S process, set in order. The set-in-order phase of 5S takes the most time and effort. One reason for that is the time required for tool board planning and creation, which can be quite tedious. However, this is the step in the process where the tangible and visual elements in your factory begin to emerge. Do not short-change this activity; take the time to get it right.

VISUAL TOOL BOARDS OR SHADOW BOARDS

Companies starting their visual journey often get excited about the implementation of tool boards. It is important to remember that tool organization, especially on shadow boards, is done after the floor items have been positioned and the layout has been determined. These first steps are critical; if the implementation team jumps ahead to creating tool boards, they will likely have some rework to do.

Before tool boards are made, the team must also sort through the tools in the area and remove anything that is not necessary. Tools can accumulate over time and become expensive to replace, repair, and keep track of. Identify the bare minimum for the work area, and organize based on that minimum. Organizing tools to the level of detail described in this book takes considerable time. Since the implementation phase can become quite tedious, with all those tools needing to be mounted on boards, outlined, labeled, and cleaned, you do not want to run the risk of having to deal with more tools than are needed in the area, nor do you want to devote a larger work area to keeping them organized. Inadequate sorting can create a considerable domino effect of extra work and inefficiency.

Tool Board Materials

In addition to some items such as paint, double-sided tape, and Velcro tape, you will need the following key supplies to get started:

- Pegboard: Generically known as perforated hardboard, pegboard is typically available at local hardware stores as predrilled hardboard (consisting of wood fibers, resin, and linseed oil subjected to a baking process), or it can be ordered in plastic or metal configurations. Note that standard board material is available in a few different sizes. Plastic and metal board systems hold up well in work environments where humidity or moisture can compromise the structure of the wood-based hardboard. Also, plastic and corrosion-free metal boards are especially well suited for any operation involving zero tolerance for undesirable airborne or washed away particulate.

- Peg Hooks: Also known as "pegs," these are typically available at your local hardware store. Start with a general peg hook assortment that is compatible with your selected board type, and then create an inventory in the kaizen box of the most desirable peg hooks. Once team members become familiar with both the virtues and limitations of each peg hook, it becomes clear which ones will best satisfy a specific tool or shadow board need.

- Peg Anchors: These do just what the name suggests: they affix or anchor the peg to the pegboard. From the several types of anchors on the market, choose one that is readily available and works with your particular board type. The anchor makes it twice as nice to hang and remove tools because it keeps the peg firmly and securely in place. Not every peg type will work with a standard anchor. In those cases you may have to customize by drilling a small hole and attaching the peg with a screw or using a plastic tie-wrap to secure the peg.

- Paint Pens: Used mainly to draw a shadow around each tool. However, when a clearly visible label cannot be attached to the tool, the paint pen can also be used to mark the tool with its particular tool board address.

- Label Maker: When stencils and paint are not a viable option for signage, printed labels can work well. From professionally printed labels with adhesive backs to sheets printed on your printer and laminated in your office, these work just fine in communicating a location and item identification; they also communicate your standard of excellence.

Designing and Constructing a Tool Board

Remember that the intention behind tool boards is to allow tools to be placed vertically on upright boards where they are clearly visible and easily accessible, keeping work surfaces clear. When designing a tool or shadow board, please understand that the board's layout will most likely need to be reevaluated each time a change in the nature of work content occurs. That does not mean the tool board will need to change each time, but it is important to assess any change in work, whether it be changing over to a new product configuration, implementing a process improvement, or simply complying with a newly released engineering change order. The tool board layout needs to be as agile as the rest of the factory resources.

Here are the steps for creating a tool board:

1. Paint the board: Any color will work. We have seen red, yellow, black, blue, green, and orange tool boards. In fact, colored pegboard is available for purchase; you pay a little more up front but save on the painting step. (My personal favorite is the industrial gray diamond plate look.)

2. Create a rough tool layout: Once the tool boards are dry, place them on the floor, a tabletop, or another flat surface and lay out all the appropriate tools and supplies on the board. Remember, these boards are excellent for holding not just tools but also materials, tape, scissors, calculators, clipboards, and other shop necessities. Your supply box should contain peg hooks, double-sided tape, Velcro tape, and other items designed to hold things vertically. As you make decisions about where items should be placed on the board, take the hanging mechanism into consideration. Also, allow extra room to draw an outline around each tool and to place labels between the tools. At this point, you are creating a rough design for your board layout to identify how much board surface will be needed to hold the workstation's supplies.

3. Cut the board: Now, remove the tools from the board, and cut a square or rectangular piece of board, sized to accommodate the footprint of the workstation tools, parts, and materials it is expected to hold. Also make sure that it will fit in the allocated space.

4. Install the tool board: Construct a wood frame for your board, using 1 inch by 1 inch studs. The board needs to float at least 1 inch from the wall or surface on which it will be mounted, so that the peg hooks will have the necessary clearance to lock into place. Walls are the logical choice for tool boards, but actually these boards can be placed anywhere: the side of a workbench or cabinet, the back of a heating, ventilating, and air conditioning (HVAC) unit, or on casters (wheels) for mobility. Just be sure that the board is visible and accessible at the point of use and does not impede or disrupt the flow of product or work.

5. Hang the items: Now it is time to hang the tools and supplies on the tool board, leaving room to place name labels between the items and to draw an outline or shadow around each item. This process is relatively slow, but it is the key to a successful tool board and 5S implementation. You may struggle through a couple of iterations before

you settle on a layout that best meets the needs of the team. Once you have it set up, encourage all those who work in the area to provide feedback and recommend changes. Here are some tips for refining the board layout and hanging the tools:

a. Include everything. Find a home on the tool board for every work item needed, including, for example, the pen used to fill out a quality form, or the calculator used in the work area. Assuming the 5S sorting activity has been successfully completed in the area (as described in Chapter 2), only the correct number of tools should remain. Rarely, a work area may need multiples of a given item. Try to avoid double stacking duplicate items on the same peg hook. Give each item its own unique location. Tool boards can accommodate most, if not all, of the tool types required to support the flow of work in the production area.

b. Consider tool size and weight. Try to locate the larger and heavier hand tools lower on the board, making sure they will not touch the floor. This is a safe approach, since it minimizes the effort needed to move heavier tools to and from the work area and reduces the risk that a large or heavy item will fall on the person retrieving the tool. Lighter tools can go up higher on the board but should stay well within ergonomic reach.

c. Sequence the tools. The most frequently used tools are normally placed nearest the point of use. Placing tools in a sequence that mirrors the order in which they are used may also make sense for your application. In other words, when the first step in a documented procedure calls for screwdriver "SD123," place screwdriver "SD123" first in your tool sequence on the tool board. Likewise, if diagonal cutter "DC1A" is required for the second process step, place it strategically in the second position on the tool board, and continue until the entire process is accounted for.

6. Create tool shadows and labels: After hanging the tools on the board, use paint pens of a contrasting color to trace an outline of each tool on the board. Time-consuming? Yes. Worthwhile? Yes. The painted outline is highly visible when the tool has been removed for use or is missing. Next, make a name label for each item, and place the label near the item's location on the board.

7. Name and address the tool boards: Give each tool board a designation, such as M5 (Maintenance area board number 5), J7 (Building J tool board number 7), or L3 (Lamination tool board 3). Label the tools

FIGURE 4.1
Work area tool board.

with their designated board's address so that everyone in the facility will know the location to which a tool should be returned.

Figures 4.1 and 4.2 show an example of a tool board that was built using these guidelines.

Personal Tools: Dilemma or Solution?

An ongoing challenge regarding tool management within many manufacturing companies is that maintenance workers are often required to supply some or all of their tools. The tools are workers' personal property, and when they leave, so do the tools. While tool boards make sense for company-owned, community-use tools, what can be done with personal tools? This issue is almost always raised during a 5S implementation. One common notion is that a company cannot set policy regarding the use or

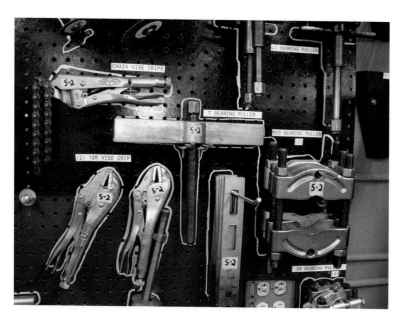

FIGURE 4.2
Work area tool board, close-up.

storage of workers' personal tools. Even though we recognize both the fine points and the emotion often accompanying both sides of this argument, it is important to keep the overall company perspective in mind. Although the tools are not owned by the company, consider the following:

1. Who owns the floor space on which the tool chest is located? The company does.
2. Who pays for the time spent sifting through piles of tools in personal tool chests? The company does.

Whether the company owns workers' tools, the business's time and money (labor hours) are directly tied to technicians' use and storage of personal tools. Disorganization and improper use of facility space causes waste, which equates to loss of profit, which equates to loss of jobs.

When workers begin to see the value of the reduced clutter and the greater efficiency in locating needed or missing tools that comes with the use of tool boards, they will often embrace the Lean philosophy. To reduce excess, they will begin to take their unnecessary tools home, separate their tools into categories, and designate specific drawers in their tool chests. They will label their drawers and cabinets for easy identification of the contents. Some technicians will even take this concept further and develop "shadow drawers." Clear location and designation within a drawer provides better organization and allows technicians to easily see when a tool is missing. Start applying Lean in manufacturing facility, and encourage your technicians to take the lead with their own personal equipment. For most, the idea will catch on, and they will begin to take pride in their ability to organize their personal tools as well as the company's tools.

Tool Check Cards

A great idea for controlling tools is to create tool check cards that are used as an instant communicator of tool status. The 5S approach to tools is the organizational phase. It also allows for quick retrieval and quick notification if a tool is missing or in use. Once the tool has been removed for whatever reason, all the shadow tells you is that it is missing—not its actual status and who has it. Tool check cards can provide that additional information (Figure 4.3).

To create a tool check card system, first identify which operators or workers will be allowed to access and to use the tools in a given work area. You will need to make several cards for each worker, in case they need to check

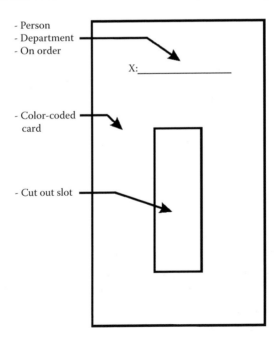

FIGURE 4.3
Tool check card.

out more than one tool at a time. Typically, three cards for each worker will suffice. You can color code the cards for workers, or make a space for their names. Design the cards so they can hang on a peg, laminate them, and place them on or near the tool board.

When workers retrieve a tool, they simply place the tool check card on the peg. Now, the whole area knows who has the tool. You can also make check cards for any management or other support personnel that may need to use a tool specific to that work area. It is also smart to make tool check cards to communicate that the tool is broken or on order.

POSITIONING TOOLS OVERHEAD

Following the creation of an overall Lean factory layout, as discussed in Chapter 3, the Lean focus often turns to the specific area in and adjacent to the production assembly line (or the workstation, line segment, workcell, or machine) around which the flow of product is physically organized. This means assessing how well assistive devices are located, positioned, and otherwise configured to promote the flow of value-adding work and reduce the waste created by excessive human motion or parts travel. This assessment may occur as a part of the original 5S activity or after the initial event; either way, the notion of set in order to promote the flow of work is paramount here.

For many movable production tools, presenting tools overhead may work well. Tools positioned overhead are easily accessible to the operator or inspector at the point of use. An articulating arm can be used to support the weight of the unit so that the operator can easily move into and out of the work envelope. Some examples where overhead presentation of tools can be used include the following:

- Mechanical assembly
  - Pneumatic driver for fasteners (automatic or manual feed with calibrated torque settings)
  - Air nozzle (but note that Lean factories avoid using costly compressed air to "blow" off debris, and most Lean practitioners have moved to a vacuum system with collection features for debris control)
- Metal, wood, and polymer surface finishing
  - Powered grinders, polishers, sanders
  - Surface finish gauges

- Machining
  - Rotary deburring tools
  - Computed numerically controlled (CNC) deburring devices (may be housed in the tool magazine)
- Manual electrical assembly (yes, some folks still have manual electronic assembly operations)
  - Temperature-controlled soldering iron
  - Flux applicator
  - Solder remover
  - Surface mount technology (SMT) placement assist devices
- Semiautomatic and automatic electrical assembly
  - Solder wave thermal probe for flow soldering axial and radial non-SMT components
- Inspection devices (for collecting both variables and attributes data)
  - Electronics: voltage, continuity, and ampere meters, oscilloscopes, signal generators, and radiofrequency (RF) signal strength meters
  - Metals: digital and vernier calipers, surface finish, hardness tester, ferrite meter, and other dimensional measurement tools tied to statistical control databases
  - Mechanical assembly: for example, torque gauges, micrometers, rulers, go/no-go templates
  - Painting and plastics: spectrometers
  - Flashlight
- Identification marker and engraver

These devices may require overhead power sources (alternating current [AC] or direct current [DC] electricity, compressed air, hydraulic, thermal, or water). Securing the mount for these items above the workstation also allows utility lines to run overhead, eliminating trip hazards at floor level.

Ensure safe operation and handling by considering the following when planning for overhead presentation of tools:

- Operating specifications (meeting part torque and tolerance, bits for fastener engagement head type, operating temperatures, humidity, noise, RF interference, and depth requirements)
- Articulation (achieving specified distances, rotation, and required force requirements) compared with normal human motion
- Weight requirements (how heavy a tool load can be handled)

Normally, these tools are ergonomically designed and sold for safe human use (weight, grip, and have designed-in safety protection). Always check the manufacturer's recommendations for safe use prior to implementing.

RIGHT-SIZING

Sometimes an actual physical tool board is not the answer you are looking for, yet the concept of the tool board is still applicable. For larger and heavier tools, such as larger drill motors, power saws, and hoists typically found in maintenance areas, open-front cabinets that are right-sized (customized) to maximize the use of vertical space are typically a good selection. Many of these tools would be too heavy to be placed on a tool board, yet the same location and item identification methods are used. Figures 4.4, 4.5, and 4.6 show before and after examples of a right-sized tool implementation.

FIGURE 4.4
Cabinet before right-sizing.

How Much Space Are You Using?

At a company where I had recently been promoted to the role of manufacturing engineering manager, the company's president (and founder) would visit the facility where I worked about two to three times per year. I looked forward to his visits earnestly but also somewhat fearfully. He was a seasoned industrial engineer from the WWII generation and was very knowledgeable, but he could be quite critical. He always wanted to walk the production floor with me after he finished visiting with the plant manager. He never came right out and said what he was thinking, speaking with simple comments and questions. Over time, I came to understand that this approach was his way of teaching.

Our factory employed about 800 people, with many of our production operations (injection molding, sheet metal, electrical assembly, subcomponent assembly, final assembly, and packaging) located within the 100,000 square foot facility. The president had subscribed to the notion of vertically integrating all aspects of the manufacturing processes when growing the business—not just within the company but under one roof when possible. We were a high-volume electronics original equipment manufacturer (OEM) production operation, and we were always struggling to achieve the increasingly higher goals of lower production costs along with a higher level of quality. In addition, we spent an undue amount of effort attempting to meet delivery commitments as new products were being introduced and older products were working their way toward the latter part of their life cycle. It was a very competitive environment, and we needed to leverage every available competitive advantage.

The first time the president walked with me through the factory, he mostly observed as I spoke. I did not really know what his purpose was. When we were done, he said, "It looks like you are effectively using only about 20% of the available space in this facility." After asking me what exactly my role was, he left.

I was unsure of what exactly he meant by his comment. Nevertheless, with my team of engineers and technicians, we proceeded to look for ways to make better use of the available space. During his next visit, I was proud to show him everything we had accomplished. As we walked from one area to the next, he seemed genuinely pleased. Yet at the end of the visit, he said, "It looks like you are using only about 25% of the available space in this facility."

It may have taken two visits, but it finally dawned on me what he was talking about. He was not talking just about using floor space but was asking me to use all space more efficiently—both horizontal and vertical space. His lessons have stayed with me all these years.

Our manufacturing engineering group embarked on initiative after initiative to improve the usage of space. We studied the details as to how every cubic foot of space in that facility was being used. Interestingly, the lessons we learned from our combined activities reached far beyond the simple usage of space. Over the next few months we evaluated every production process and how we could improve the flow of materials between areas. The process evaluations led to the implementation of a factory-level performance measurement based on all the discrete manufacturing processes. The information we collected led us to making process improvement decisions, which in turn yielded favorable results. The president's ability to refocus our energies simply by making a comment also taught us quite a bit about leadership technique, too.

Our first-pass quality acceptance rates began to increase dramatically, and our production costs dropped. We opened up a large section of floor space by removing the work-in-progress (WIP) queue between operations and by removing an entire production line dedicated to rework; we simply did not need it anymore. We also began to hit our delivery commitments to customers.

On his next visit, as we walked around the facility, he said with a smile, "It looks like you're using only about 40% of the available space." Right then and there, I knew we were on the right track.

This anecdote makes the case for right-sizing. If an item is needed (a tool, inventoried part, or consumable) to support production activities, it may need to be stored, but why not in a location that has been right-sized for it (including the use of vertical storage).

Some plant managers argue that it is a waste of time and money to customize a storage location for tools or materials. It is true that using standardized shelving may have a lower initial cost and create a sense of

FIGURE 4.5
Cabinet after right-sizing.

modularity for future uses. However, look at the vacant space between shelves in a typical standardized shelving unit. Some managers settle for the wasted space in this storage model because there are insufficient internal driving forces to change it. Only when the need for more floor space is identified does the notion of using vertical storage to save space arise.

The right-sizing concept applies even to companies that use vertical carousels to improve the storage density of various items—only in the inverse. Vertical carousels can also minimize the time required to store and retrieve raw material, parts, and fixtures. But there may be a trade-off between optimum access time (i.e., where an item is stored relative to the pick point) and optimum density of storage (i.e., which storage location can best accommodate the item physically). There are often opportunities to better use the available space by right-sizing the item being stored to the physical size of the carousel's storage location.

The Lean argument centers around the cost of floor space right now—as in today—to provide for a new product line, for instance, or the cost of the time it takes when production employees must repeatedly attempt to

FIGURE 4.6
Workbench after right-sizing.

access a tool or part that is hidden behind or underneath other "stuff." It is a matter of deciding between the cost of one-time customization versus the cost of ongoing, repetitive waste of time and effort.

Either way, you must choose your stance on right-sizing based on the primary driving factors in your operation.

5

Visual Parts and Supplies

Applied correctly, visual management techniques can have a profound impact on a company's inventory levels. Cases from actual companies have shown that purchased inventory levels can be reduced by millions of dollars while maintaining production that meets customer demand. In addition to the materials consumed in the manufacture of an end product, consumables such as gloves, glues, solvents, rags, tapes, cutters, mills, welding rod, and similar supplies also have been minimized dramatically. These companies have been able to convert warehouse space into value-added production operations. For smaller companies, the total dollar amounts are not as staggering, but the positive impacts are just as favorable.

Before you pull the materials manager aside and tell him or her to start drawing down inventory levels, consider this: when a company carries inventories of raw materials, purchased parts, and purchased subassemblies at levels higher than what it has planned orders for, look beyond the materials manager; it probably was not his or her decision.

INVENTORY BASICS

Let's start by exploring a few questions about inventory.

When We Use the Term *Inventory*, What Specifically Are We Talking About?

A simplified way of looking at inventory in the physical sense is to see it as the summation of the following:

1. Raw materials, purchased parts, and subassemblies
2. Work in process (WIP)
3. Finished goods inventory
4. Consumables (or supplies)

Physical inventory also requires physical space to store it. Effective use of the physical space is a key concern in Lean efforts. Reducing the amount of inventory a company stores means reducing the amount of space required for the stockroom.

On the other hand, inventory is also measured in dollars. To the manufacturing accountant, inventory is the aggregate dollar amount representing the value of every item in its various forms throughout the company. In any business, the approval to issue a purchase order represents someone's strategic decision as to how the company's money will be allocated. For accountants, it makes little sense to spend money on an item that does not get used. Yet each year most accounting managers write off amounts representing obsolete, scrapped, and other unused or unusable inventory. Every dollar not spent on unneeded inventory (or anything else unnecessary) is one more dollar available for another company purpose. Have we not all, more than once, overheard the question, "I wonder why this item was purchased in the first place?"

Why Is Having More Inventory than What Is Needed to Support Customer Demand a Bad Thing?

There are many reasons companies carry more inventory than what is needed to meet current and forecasted customer demand. Given the challenges of the emerging global supply streams, pointing to the uncertainties of delivery and quality performance by suppliers, many material managers are being asked to "stock up" as a preventive measure.

On the flip side, carrying excess inventory is a burden on the company's bottom line. The increasingly competitive world of manufacturing dictates that we must find ways to reduce costs. Carrying extra inventory is no longer a discretionary luxury for most companies. We must ensure that all required materials are available to support customer demand, yet at the same time we must find ways to right-size inventory levels—freeing up cash for other investment. Otherwise, funding needed to support a new product development activity or a new capital purchase may have to be delayed, or the need for cash may force the company to borrow funds. In addition, the space used to warehouse inventory is expensive—representing a healthy portion of the cost of the inventory. If excess parts are cleared out or stored more efficiently, the area may be used to house a new value-adding production operation. Would it not be nice to avoid new construction costs by simply better using existing floor space?

Why Does Your Company Carry Its Existing Levels of Inventory?

Oftentimes we hear the following reasons (made by individuals in the positions noted) for a company carrying excess inventory in the stockroom. Perhaps you can add another reason or two to the list.

- "A master schedule does not exist here; therefore, excess materials are brought in to cover our 'best guess' for parts needed to meet anticipated product sales." (materials manager)
- "I simply feel more comfortable having higher levels of inventory; it gives me a sense of having another insurance policy for the business." (business owner and company president)
- "Production scrap rates are so variable we need to carry more parts to cover the unplanned losses." (purchasing and production managers)
- "Many suppliers are unreliable in meeting delivery commitments." (materials manager)
- "We order the minimum order quantity to get the best per-item price." (purchasing manager, vice president of operations, owner)
- "Our suppliers and distributors are no longer willing to carry extra inventory for us." (purchasing manager)
- "Even though the part is obsolete, we may design it back into our product line someday." (engineering manager)
- "Engineering had us order these parts thinking we would use them on a future product." (materials manager)
- "Even though we sold that machine years ago, I'm told we have to keep the spare parts here on the shelf." (maintenance manager)

Of course, each statement reflects both the emerging trends of the worldwide supply base as well as the strategic thinking of some owners and senior managers regarding safe materials management. Likewise, we can read into the comments the unforgiving nature and absolute need for having enough of the correct parts on hand to ensure the production and shipment of a customer's order. However, if embraced in their entirety, Lean business methods can help provide a different mind-set and a new backdrop to help resolve or contain nearly every concern previously noted.

Is It Possible to Drive Down Inventory Levels without Putting Production and Shipping Commitments in Jeopardy?

Let's be clear: Lean is not about starving production of the parts it needs. Lean is about addressing excess, wherever it may be. Lean is about ensuring that parts are available as needed to meet demand. For companies who have not already started down this path, opportunities to draw down inventory levels are normally plentiful.

What Role Does a Visual Management System Play in Achieving a Reduced Inventory Level?

Visual tools are used to indicate and communicate the need for parts and consumable supplies, including both the demand from a production area to the stock room as well as the demand from the stockroom to the suppliers and vendors.

Visual tools are also used to communicate and help the materials team manage issues with the supply function, including the following:

- Supplier and vendor performance
- Materials team performance
- Part-specific issues

A FEW GENERAL POINTS ON SUPPLY CHAIN MANAGEMENT

Before we delve into more detailed information on setting up visual parts and supplies inventory, let's review a few overall supply chain management issues that are operative in management of suppliers and inventory generally: the role of manufacturing software systems, current global supply chain trends, and the role of receiving inspection.

The Role of Manufacturing Software Systems

Many business owners or senior managers complain that their manufacturing software (material requirements planning [MRP] or enterprise resource planning [ERP] system) is "holding them hostage." Actually, when set up and used correctly, these systems are excellent financial accounting tools—and can be of great assistance to everyone else.

For larger companies, these systems provide product structure, inventory, and costing information to sales, engineering, purchasing, materials, quality, planning, scheduling, and production managers. They handle the complexity of multiple part numbers while synchronizing demand with the correct timing for completing a multilevel bill of materials (BOM) and capturing the effective dates for pending and released engineering changes. These systems can normally create accurate demand information for purchasing, planning, and manufacturing. Most systems are, in fact, quite sophisticated and very powerful, especially when handling a vast quantity of part numbers.

Whether for a large, medium-sized, or small manufacturing company, a system complementary to the Lean manufacturing model should be a "pull"-based, versus a "push"-based, system. Better yet is to leverage a well-conceived kanban system to improve the flow of product through your production facilities.

These software-based systems do an even better job when a master schedule reflecting a company's business plan is kept current and functioning properly. However, most companies lack an accurate and up-to-date master schedule, which is a contributing factor to carrying more inventory than necessary.

Current Global Trends

Global trends for suppliers and distributors seem to indicate that an inventory draw-down is occurring across most market segments. In other words, you are not alone. The recent economic crisis has underscored for many producers and distributors the cost of carrying too much inventory. To enjoy a continuation of supplier- or vendor-held inventory is probably going to require some investment of time and money on your part. A long-term supply agreement with some sort of upfront financial commitment will be required to see this practice continue. Not every supplier or vendor will be willing to offer this option. However, not all control is lost.

Using visual management tools, you can measure and report the performance of your company's suppliers and vendors. Visual indicators will communicate when a pricing, delivery, or quality issue arises. Granted, you have more leverage when multiple suppliers are vying for your orders. But when action is required on your part, you have the visual management system in place to keep the performance information in front of you and your entire team.

Receiving Inspection

Does the act of inspecting incoming parts and supplies add value? Absolutely not—not even in the most liberal of Lean definitions. Yet receiving inspection can preserve value and prevent the costly practice of waiting to discover a noncompliant item only after it has made its way into the value-adding processes.

Until historical statistical evidence shows sufficient supplier process control is in place to support the decision that incoming inspection is no longer warranted, compliance to specification must be verified. The cost of finding a nonconforming product on receipt is normally far smaller than after it has made its way into the process and has resulted in a defective product. The time spent making the defective product has been lost, and the time and cost to rework or scrap it adds up quickly. In addition, the cost of transportation back to the supplier is a real charge.

Many companies use a form of source inspection: inspectors located at the supplier's production location to verify compliance and prevent nonconforming product from ever leaving their factory. Reliable source inspection data can be used to reduce or eliminate incoming inspection.

A TOUR THROUGH THE IDEAL STOCKROOM

With those background issues covered, let's move on to visualizing a visual stockroom. First, how does your warehouse or stockroom currently look? How well does it work? Perhaps not as well as you would like. Let's take a walk through an ideal (perhaps imaginary) stockroom. Patricia, the stockroom supervisor, will show us around.

Materials Common Area

First of all, we can see the area outside the stockroom is neat and clean. The area outside the room is the materials common area, which is in impeccable order, with lines and visible location numbers painted on the cement floor. Corresponding location identifications are also found on the wall above each location.

As we look closer, one of the first things we notice are two small vending machines. Even though there are other such vending machines located throughout the plant near the point of their use, the items dispensed here are used by various employees from different areas who pass this way.

As we watch, a production employee walks up to one machine and swipes his employee ID along with a work order number printed on a card; both are verified before the machine dispenses the desired item in the quantity requested. The information becomes a recordable transaction for accounting, purchasing, and the vendor. When a reorder point is reached, the inventory in each vending machine will be replenished by the vendor directly, leaving stockroom personnel to focus on items of greater value.

Stockroom Entrance

The next thing we notice is that the stockroom has a secure entrance, allowing access to authorized personnel only. There is a checkout booth for material handling personnel retrieving parts needed for delivery to production. Visual graphics depict the proper steps for employees to follow when checking out and returning parts and tools.

Before we enter the stockroom, we also notice four information boards near the door labeled "SUPPLIERS," "VENDORS," "PROBLEM PARTS," "MATERIALS TEAM." Patricia explains that her company differentiates between suppliers and vendors: suppliers are companies that produce value-added items in accordance with company-supplied specifications; vendors provide commodity products.

These information boards display a "Top Ten" list. For the suppliers and vendors, each list has four columns to the right of a column labeled "Company Name." The column titles are "Quality," "Delivery," "Pricing," and "Comments." To the right of each company's name we notice either a green, amber, or red magnetic dot, indicating recent performance. Patricia explains that the materials manager has specific criteria supporting the justification for the placement of each color; these visual dots create an immediate message for all to see. For one company on the list, Patricia points out the red dot under the quality heading, as well as the Comments column, where it notes that her company is a sole supplier for a critical part with which it is currently having problems. (Note: Many "sole supplier" situations, in contrast to "sole vendor" relationships, present special reasons for extra care and attention.)

The "Problem Parts" list is a list of the top 10 problem items used in manufacturing; it follows the same basic format as the Suppliers list, except that in this case the first column is labeled "Part Number/Description," and the Comments column depicts the status of any correction action being taken by the supplier or vendor.

The "Materials Team" board shows the status of metrics that are critically important to the company. This board is slightly different, showing "Turns" at the macro level and then how their "Inventory" dollars compare with team goals. Where there are variances between goals and actual performance, the Comments column offers an explanation.

These four boards in the materials common area visually depict, within a few seconds for anyone walking by, the status of the key factors in the supply stream. They are updated frequently.

Patricia now brings us into the stockroom. As we enter, we notice that the storage locations are carefully marked and obviously well organized. We do not see opened boxes, box knives, or tape sitting around anywhere. Stockroom tools are placed on tool boards, complete with neatly drawn shadows and easy-to-read labeling.

Unloading Dock

Patricia suggests that we start at the unloading dock, where the whole process begins. The unloading dock is an incoming parts staging area located at one end of the stockroom to provide for the controlled flow of parts entering the facility. There are two areas marked "Unloading" and "Returns." Both areas are clearly identified for all delivery drivers to see. In fact, each carrier has a specific area labeled with its name and with lines painted on the floor. The "Returns" area contains only one package. Patricia notes that the efforts of the materials team in working closely with suppliers and vendors has really helped reduce the number of returns. A return material authorization (RMA) form is attached to the package, ready for the delivery driver's pick-up. She says that the delivery drivers have enjoyed the gold stars on the "Delivery" performance board that reward them for deliveries and paperwork completed correctly and in a timely manner.

Most but not all parts are delivered directly to the unloading dock. Some items are actually delivered to a specific, well-marked location within the factory.

The unloading area serves as a checkpoint for the verification of paperwork. When asked if this is where the "parts" are "received," Patricia quickly responds that the "receive" function happens later in the material process when every package, box, or item is identified with a stamp, label, or traveler as it enters the facility. The information on the label helps everyone see which material steps are required and which have been successfully completed for each item.

For this materials group, delivery verification proves only that an item has been delivered against an issued purchase order and that the label lists the correct part number and quantity. We watch as Patricia completes this process with a quick electronic scan that immediately verifies the delivery as correct and indicates that no receiving inspection is required for any of the package contents.

If an item is not flagged for inspection, it is entered into the company's enterprise-wide system as received, and then it is moved to its identified inventory location—in the stockroom, on the production floor, or in the yard. The person handling the part orients it exactly as it will be needed in production. In fact, if the item is delivered straight to manufacturing by a supplier, the supplier orients it so that it is ready to go into the production process. A simple green dot or mark is placed on the box or part to indicate it has successfully completed the receiving process and who completed the process.

Receiving Inspection Area

When asked how the receiving inspection flagging process works, Patricia picks up another box she knows has been flagged. When she scans the item label, a message window appears on her monitor showing that receiving inspection is required for the contents of the package.

The purpose of flagging items for inspection at receiving is to verify that each item's critical measurements meet engineering specification and that the quantity of items matches the purchase order. Patricia marks the flagged package with a yellow dot indicating it is awaiting inspection as she moves the item into the secure receiving inspection area. A simple system transaction communicates that the parts have been delivered and are now located in the receiving inspection area. After passing inspection, the item is marked with the inspector's "inspection" stamp and recorded on the quality record, and the transaction is entered into the system. The item can now be given a green dot and moved to its inventory location; in this case, the traveler will also include the receiving inspection information. If the item fails inspection, a red dot is placed on it, marking it for handling in accordance with the company's quality policy.

Main Stockroom

We leave the incoming inspection area and enter the inner workings of the greater stockroom, where parts are stored in locations that waste little vertical or horizontal space. Heavy items are stored down low, with lighter items up higher. Items with a higher demand are placed closer to the point of demand. Each inventory location is identified with a fixed placard, indicating the part number and minimum, maximum, and reorder quantity levels. This is where the accountant's physical inventory is periodically verified. From a manufacturing standpoint, it is critical never to shut the process down due to lack of parts. Conversely, an accurate part count is critical to the company financial reports.

This inventory system is set up on a kanban model. The stockroom employee can see if a part is ready for reorder simply by noticing when the order point indicator becomes visible. The process is quite simple. Even though there may be complex calculations supporting the creation of each reorder point and the reorder quantity, the simple reorder indicator line makes all the figuring transparent.

Patricia explains that the company is considering adding a vertical carousel to take advantage of more vertical space and to reduce the time to retrieve specific parts.

As we exit this visual stockroom, we are impressed with Patricia's knowledge of the process, the simplicity of the kanban systems, and the overwhelming sense that inventory levels are set in balance with the need to replenish what is being consumed by manufacturing.

Stockroom Layout Considerations

Our tour with Patricia highlighted many of the key features in an ideal layout for a stockroom. In a nutshell, orderly and efficient inventory storage takes into account several factors.

Factory Destination

Where is the point of use? A company does not have to have just one stockroom. If you must inventory parts, it is best to store them as close as possible to where they are consumed. It may become a decision that involves the cost of floor space versus the cost of positioning transaction terminals away from the stockroom. In any case, the kanban card will have the item's location printed on it to provide clear instruction when replenishment activity is under way.

Size and Weight

How big is the item? Larger items require special handling. Since transporting any part unnecessarily is wasted movement, transporting large parts unrelated to the value-adding process is an abomination because of the effort expended to move them. In addition, how much does the item weigh? Can a person handle it in a cart, will a forklift be needed, or will an overhead crane be necessary to move it?

Demand Volume

How many parts are consumed on a periodic basis? If the volume is high enough, an automatic delivery system may be warranted. If demand for the part is, say, one per year, that is a whole different story. Higher-volume parts (not necessarily parts like resisters and capacitors) can be considered the same as one large part. The number of times you move the parts adds up and over time will surely equate to one large item. Store them within reach for easy and rapid movement to production.

INVENTORY REDUCTION STRATEGY

As mentioned earlier, inventory for an accountant is a dollar amount representing the cost of all purchased raw materials and parts in stock plus the value of all products in a manufacturing process (WIP) plus the value of all end products (finished goods) that have not yet been shipped or invoiced. The accounting function normally requires a periodic snapshot verification of what inventory is physically present. An accurate inventory dollar amount helps establish baselines for Lean activities.

From our perspective, these three basic forms of physical inventory represent important steps in the value stream, leading to customer order fulfillment. Therefore, all inventory functions present opportunities for 5S implementation and waste removal. Materials management is a key role in any manufacturing company. A successful materials group will ensure that raw material, purchased parts, and manufactured subcomponents, all of which meet engineering specifications, are systematically and readily made available to meet production demand. Pretty simple, isn't it? All we need are the correct parts, in the right quantity, in the time frame we need them.

As mentioned previously, the purpose of inventory reduction is not to reduce quantities to insufficient levels that will halt the production process; rather, it is to reduce quantities to an appropriate level that allows for smart replenishment, promotes visibility of potential inventory issues, increases working capital, and opens up floor space. This section covers the key visual management strategies for achieving those ends and discusses the most efficient methods of delivering parts to your value-adding processes to reduce inefficiency and to promote more effective production.

5S and Kanban

A Lean stockroom in a manufacturing company is a primary control mechanism for incoming materials, parts, and supplies. However, the materials function is also a key player in the internal distribution of product consumed by the value-adding production activities, including delivering parts to points of demand in the Lean factory.

You are now quite familiar with the concept of 5S and with visual tool boards. 5S implementation should be considered an important initiative for all inventory locations, just as it was for work areas. Kanban is a visual management tool used in various ways, in every aspect of Lean manufacturing. In inventory and material management, a kanban is both a signal that more material is needed in production and an indication that something needs to be ordered. We will focus on these two Lean techniques in the stockroom: 5S and kanban.

5S in the Stockroom

The layout of stockroom inventory is important to its functionality as well as to aesthetics and organization. The layout should be determined based on the most appropriate flow and function. Here are the essential locations and areas:

- Incoming parts staging
- Receiving inspection
- Raw material inventory
- Subassembly inventory
- Finished goods inventory
- Supplies and tools areas
- Parts for production

Incoming Parts Staging

Purchased raw materials, discrete parts, and subassemblies require a secure staging area near or in the Lean stockroom that allows for the contents of each delivery to be verified for correct part numbering and quantity. The area should have provisions for appropriate levels of security, with limited access.

The designated area can be a specific place on the floor or a specified shelf in the room. Incoming staging areas will vary in size, depending on the type of parts. Keep the size and quantity of parts in mind when identifying the appropriate space for your staging area. Mark this area with floor tape and label it accordingly, on the floor as well as overhead or on the walls.

The incoming parts staging area, or "delivery" area, should be highly visible to anyone entering the stockroom and should be treated as a quarantine area. In addition to its primary function, this area also provides great visual management. A staging area that begins to fill to capacity is an indication that parts are not being processed as planned, that parts are being purchased too early or in excessive quantities, or that work issues may exist in the production or repair areas.

Returning parts to vendors and suppliers can be a common occurrence. Hopefully, the returns are not due to quality issues. Since returning parts to suppliers is a function of the stockroom, a small area or shelf should be reserved for this purpose. A visible, easily identifiable area for damaged or unneeded parts will reduce confusion, thereby reducing motion, transportation, and mistakes. The returns area allows the supplier to easily locate the parts being returned without having to wait for a technician to assist them. Suppliers can quickly stop by your shop, check the returns area, and go about their business. The two most important factors are to designate a single area for returns and to identify it clearly with signs and labels.

Receiving Inspection

For a Lean factory to run on all cylinders, a zero-tolerance policy regarding nonconforming incoming materials must exist and be strictly adhered to. No part should leave an inventory location without being identified somehow as compliant with specifications. Login access to the company's computer system is required here. Receiving inspection is actually a function of the quality assurance team but is located in or near the delivery area to minimize excess movement of parts. For items that can be inspected only in controlled environments (e.g., temperature, airborne particulate count levels, humidity, light exposure), exceptions to the standard receiving inspection process may be required.

The formal process for receiving inspection will be documented in your company's formal quality system.

Supplies and Tools Area

The supplies area contains commodities or supply items that are used on a regular basis, such as the following:

- Rags, shop towels, and brushes
- Cleaners and solvents
- Lubricants
- Adhesives and glues
- Welding rod and wire
- Small end mills and turning tools
- Order-specific hand tools
- Other company-specific supply items

The challenge is determining the correct amount to keep on hand. For example, how many rags should you stock? How long will two boxes of 100 rags each last? With a little math, you can estimate initial usage and then monitor actual usage.

The stockroom contains supplies and materials vital to support the production operation as well as those for general use or facility maintenance.

Regardless of use, all supplies must be set up on a kanban system to monitor usage, to keep cost down, and to reduce carrying needs. A simple kanban system is discussed later in this chapter.

Parts for Production

The final function of the stockroom is to prepare parts for material handlers to deliver to the production floor. Parts for a specific work area should be placed on their own mobile setup cart with proper identification. Since you have developed an addressing system as part of your visual factory layout and have assigned a unique address for each production process, you can use the addresses on the carts for identification.

Mobile setup carts holding individual parts or kits of parts are prepared by stockroom personnel based on pick-up dates, delivery times, destination, and hierarchy of importance. Each cart should remain under stockroom control until verified as correct and removed by material handler. If you have room, establish individual spots for the setup carts, and mark them with floor tape and with floor and wall labels indicating the cart and work area number. Establish as many lanes as needed to park the setup carts. Each setup cart is assigned by number to a lane. When a cart is emptied in a work area, it is returned to the parts room, where it will be filled with a new set of parts to meet production demand. To ensure material handlers are not wasting time retrieving carts, develop a kanban system to signal the parts room for more carts.

Replenishment: Kanban and Two-Bin Systems

As discussed previously, there are two key visual replenishment systems to help you manage the flow of parts and inventory through the factory: kanban systems and two-bin systems.

Setting Up a Kanban System

Here is a simple approach to setting up a kanban system for general supplies kept in the stockroom:

1. Identify all the material and supplies needed in the stockroom.
2. Separate them into categories (e.g., fluids, adhesives, sanding, general maintenance, electrical, hardware).

3. Identify the amount to be on hand at all times. Ask this question: How much is one week's worth (assuming that time period allows for time for ordering and restocking)?
4. Identify the reorder quantity (e.g., 1 bottle, 2 boxes).
5. Decide where the supplies will be located in the parts room.
6. Implement 5S for the supplies so that each item has a home location, regardless of size.
7. Place labels to designate the item.
8. Print out kanban cards (one card for each bin location), and place them near the item (Figure 5.1).

Notice that the kanban card includes the item description and part number, the minimum quantity to be kept on hand, the maximum quantity or reorder quantity, and the kanban card number (in the right-hand corner). When the minimum quantity is reached, that is the signal for replenishment. Sometimes, another visual signal, such as a red dot under the product, can be used to indicate that the card should be submitted for replenishment. When the "signal" is present,

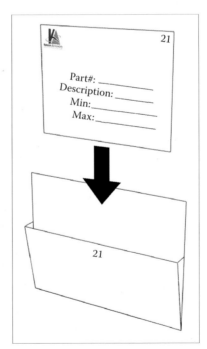

FIGURE 5.1
Kanban card.

the card should be placed into a kanban card bin. The card is now the signal to order the supply. You may want to wait until a collection of cards has accumulated, and then place the order. The kanban card number is a reference number that can be used to help track cards in a master list. Figures 5.2 through 5.7 illustrate the process. In Figure 5.6, the red signal indicates that a card has been placed in the box and is ready for pick-up.

Two-Bin Systems

The two-bin system is another visual system for managing the flow of parts. In this section, we describe a team approach to setting up a two-bin replenishment system. This activity will require about four to six team members (depending on the number of bins in the process). First, we will cover some basic information on the bins and their labeling.

Parts Bins and Color-Coded Labels

The parts bins used to supply each assembly line should be color coded to help reduce the possibility that a bin full of parts coming from the stockroom will be placed at the wrong line. For example, let's say there

FIGURE 5.2
Cards near item.

FIGURE 5.3
Card numbering system.

FIGURE 5.4
Colored DOT: Signal to replenish.

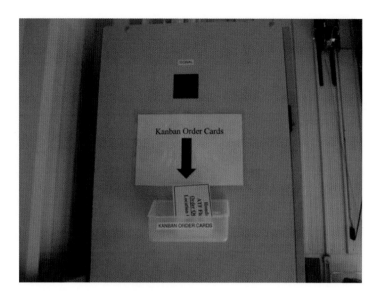

FIGURE 5.5
Remove card from sleeve and place in out box.

FIGURE 5.6
Attach signal.

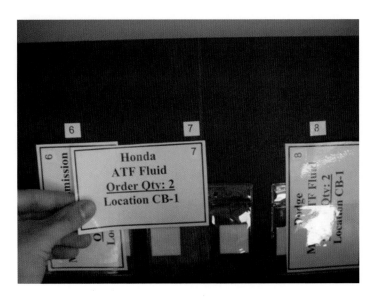

FIGURE 5.7
Return card to location.

are three assembly lines in the factory: A-line, B-line, and C-line. The A-line could have orange labels, B-line yellow labels, and C-line green labels. An orange bin placed at the C-line will be easily identified as the incorrect parts bin for that line. This method allows production supervisors, material handlers, and production personnel to see the mistake from a distance and thereby to remedy the situation much more quickly.

Some companies use colored bins instead of colored labels. This is perfectly acceptable since it serves the same purpose. As long as the bins can be associated with a particular line or workcell, the visual management of those bins and control of the parts can be accomplished.

Each label must contain the part description, part number, quantity, and the location of the assembly line, workcell, or other specific work area. Three labels are required for each part: one for each of the two bins; and one for the parts rack where the bin is located. Figure 5.8 shows an example of bin and location labels.

The bin labels are a visual aid for the material handler. Each label accurately identifies the contents of the bin. The combination of colored labels, floor designations, and workstation signs clearly identifies the location of the bins, making the parts easy to find. Figures 5.9 through 5.12 illustrate the process of a two-bin system.

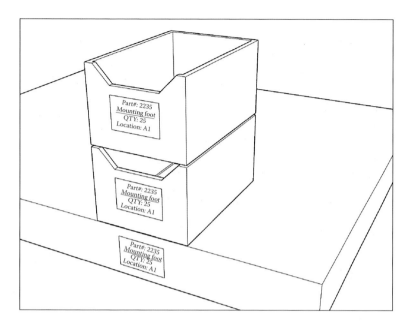

FIGURE 5.8
Two-bin system label set.

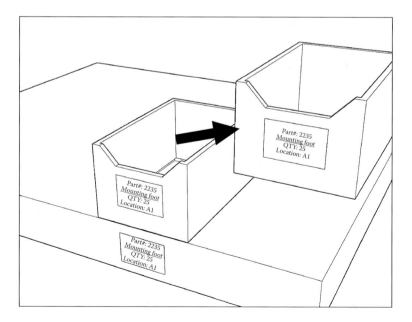

FIGURE 5.9
Two-bin system in use, step 1.

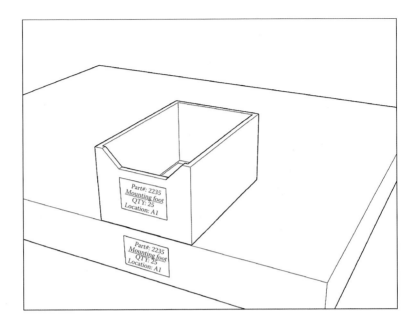

FIGURE 5.10
Two-bin system in use, step 2.

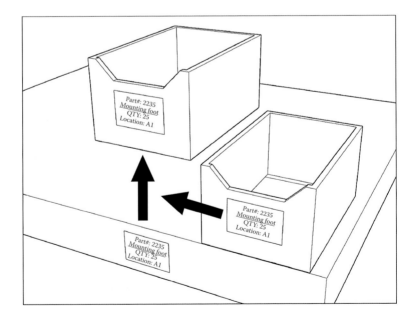

FIGURE 5.11
Two-bin system in use, step 3.

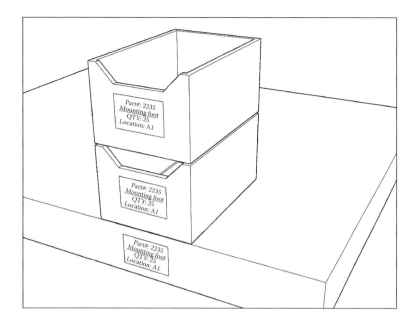

FIGURE 5.12
Two-bin system in use, step 4.

This system is highly effective, allowing material to flow easily in and out of the workstation. Material handlers and assemblers work together to ensure that parts are available when needed and that the quantity is accurate to keep the line at takt time.

Two-Bin Team Exercise

This exercise requires each team member to work on a specific task. One team member should be responsible for laminating the labels and cutting them out. Label makers work well for this exercise, as long as colored labels can be used. If colored bins are being used, the labels should be the same color.

Subassembly Build Levels

Although it may be ideal when an entire product can be built on the main assembly line, many companies have constraints that prevent this. Installing feeder lines or subassembly workcells will accomplish the task just as effectively.

For example, let's say that workcell 6 produces a subassembly of product A at a given takt time that will ensure the completed item is ready for installation on assembly line 2 when needed. However, workcell 6 also makes the small, simple, quickly built assemblies needed for product B, which is built on assembly line 1.

If proper visual aids are not in place, workcell operators may overbuild items that are not needed and will only slow down the assembly line. In situations like this, build levels should be created telling the operators when to start and stop building a given product. They can switch back and forth as a team, building only the appropriate quantities at the appropriate times. If the build levels for storage on the main assembly line have been established, these same quantities can be applied to the subassembly workcell. For example:

Large Subassembly	Quantity
Main body panel	10
Trunk	10
Small Subassembly	**Quantity**
Tool kit	24
Mirror	24
Instruction kit	24

The team leader should select team members to create and implement visual aids for the subassembly operators and for the main assembly operators. In the subassembly workcell, there are two designated racks for placing finished goods: one for in process; and one for outgoing subassemblies. Based on the aforementioned quantities, build-level signs should be made to direct the operators. Figure 5.5 shows a sign that can be used for this purpose.

The line is designed such that 24 tool kits equates to a three-hour supply. It takes 0.82 minutes, or approximately 50 seconds, to assemble a tool kit; therefore, the subassembly operator has adequate time to build the required number of kits before the material handler comes to retrieve them. The empty bin or row where the finished subassembly is located is the visual signal to start building additional kits. As long as the subassembly operators follow the build level requirements, they will not get behind or build too far ahead.

Once the Lean approach to creating a right-sized inventory is understood, the application of 5S, visual communication, kanban, and two-bin systems can help an organization reduce excess inventory to quantities that are in balance with production demand levels.

6

Visual Maintenance and Total Productive Maintenance Boards

In any factory, the maintenance team performs the significant role of preserving company fixed assets by installing, removing, altering, and maintaining both plant fixtures and equipment. The leader of this group is typically an individual with a knack for managing projects and leading people, is skilled at troubleshooting complex devices, and is an accomplished diplomat. Team members are likewise technically skilled and must multitask to accomplish critical objectives.

THE ROLE OF MAINTENANCE

Before we dive into the heart of the chapter, let's dispel two notorious pieces of accepted wisdom concerning working on the maintenance posse.

Common Misconceptions

To start, the role of providing maintenance is unique within any organization. Many production workers seek the higher pay and what they view as the loftier position of a maintenance technician. These employees will take classes at the local community college, study countless hours, and pass grueling tests to show they meet rigorous position requirements. Understandably, many newly anointed maintenance team members, who have mainly viewed maintenance from the outside, feel a sense of "graduating" from the production floor to coveted higher ground when joining this "elite" group that is seemingly not harried by the daily demands of production schedules. Many feel their aptitude simply does not resonate with the repetitive nature of the work often found in production environments.

The reality is that a company's income stream comes directly from selling value-added products produced by manufacturing; that is what provides the money to operate the business, to pay dividends to shareholders, and to pay employees' wages and salaries. Therefore, every position in the plant, no matter how we may choose to tiptoe around it, exists to support the company's mission of producing value-added products to sell. For the sales team, this means securing more orders for manufacturing to produce. Engineering and research and development (R&D) groups exist to create new products to produce and sell. Scheduling and planning groups create cohesive production plans, optimizing all resources to achieve delivery commitments. In the materials group, purchasing agents negotiate and buyers purchase all the materials necessary to support the company's ongoing operations— especially the direct materials consumed in producing value-added product. Everyone has a hand in this, including the maintenance team.

Therefore, newly ordained maintenance technicians would benefit from aligning themselves with value-adding processes and leveraging their knowledge of making things rather than attempting to escape the demands of daily production. Getting a clearer understanding of the mission and objectives of the maintenance function only solidifies a technician's ability to provide production personnel with the help they may need.

Let's be clear. The role of maintenance is not just about troubleshooting and repairing a machine or providing preventive maintenance (PM) on a piece of equipment. The job of maintenance includes every activity necessary to sustain and improve the company's fixed asset capacity to make products and thereby to make money.

Second, maintenance managers are commonly pictured with a cup of coffee in one hand and a newspaper in the other, feet resting up on the desk—all in all, with a lack of work to attend to. And, although apparently extremely competent and talented, they never get overly excited about the new idea you just came in with to save the company a bundle of money. This image is usually incorrect; these unfortunate souls are most likely wondering how they are going to fit your new project in along with everything else plant management has assigned them to do. Their behavior represents a manager besieged with an endless list of seemingly impossible tasks and unrealistic due dates on a limited budget; their actions are simply the manifestation of a defense mechanism as they attempt to deal with the seemingly impossible.

The fact is, due to the nature of the beast of protecting (creating, fixing, installing, maintaining, removing, and replacing) the buildings and equipment, most maintenance managers are saddled with a hefty load of scheduled projects and preventive maintenance activities coupled with the uncertainty of daily equipment breakdowns, and the team is usually under-resourced. No matter how the image may appear, maintenance bosses do not sit in an ivory tower; these managers simply need some guidance and help to move beyond their world of everyday crisis and settle in on some new territory of more control and predictability.

First Responder

The maintenance team fills the critical role of first responder, ensuring production stoppages are minimized or averted altogether when a piece of machinery goes down. In equipment-intensive production operations especially, maintenance technicians find themselves taking center stage whenever production is unexpectedly halted. As if these individuals do not feel sufficient pressure to determine a root cause in short order and to implement a fix just as fast, these craftsmen and craftswomen may also find themselves the target of untimely questions such as, "When will the machine be fixed?" "How did this happen?" and "Didn't you just repair this equipment yesterday?" Most forward-thinking managers have learned that interrupting a troubleshooting effort seldom, if ever, assists in getting the matter resolved sooner.

Impact of Product Nonconformities

A second major issue faced by the first responder arises when a quality problem is detected, and everyone immediately agrees it is the result of a malfunctioning machine. Often, however, hours of troubleshooting reveal the real root cause to be a workmanship blunder, a program error, or a material problem. When quantifiable data are not available, there is usually ample opinion to fill the void. There is not a faster way to diminish enthusiasm than to light a fire under someone, only to find out later it was not necessary.

When a machine is found to be the culprit, one good question to ask is, "What was the machine doing before the problem was identified?" If quantitative process control information is lacking, the question may go unanswered—forever, or until the problem resurfaces. In today's world of computed numerically controlled (CNC) machines, historical data can usually provide answers. For other types of equipment, finding event history may prove more difficult. Starting a troubleshooting effort from scratch only extends the total time it will take. Sound familiar?

In a manufacturing company where the operative culture is reactive rather than proactive, maintenance technicians become firefighters—always reacting to the current crisis—rather than planning and working to a plan. In this situation, the role of first responder equates to applying treatment for a symptom rather than finding and resolving the underlying disease.

Let's think about it for a minute. A machine breaks down in the middle of a critical production run; logic would suggest the thing to do is to levy all available resources to repair the equipment and get it back up and running, right? The obvious answer is absolutely. The less obvious and deeper question, however, is could the breakdown have been prevented? What if a more systematic approach toward caring for the equipment had been in place beforehand?

Some companies simply run a machine until it breaks, repair it, and then start producing again. This is a very expensive and inefficient way to use equipment. It is akin to not changing the oil in your car, only to find down the road that the reason your car broke down was that the engine seized up due to lack of oil. How much would that oil change have cost? The other problem with the "run them till they drop" syndrome is that it invites unplanned downtime for every machine—meaning we do not know when the equipment will fail. It is not much different from playing Russian roulette with our machinery, and it creates another variable out of our control. The sudden loss of a piece of production equipment wreaks havoc on a busy production schedule, where the looming ship date may already be in peril due to unplanned absenteeism and to problems with incoming material and workmanship. Add the mix of today's new sales order expedites, and we have a boatload of problems to overcome.

Why do we bemoan the challenges faced by a typical maintenance group? We do so because many, if not all, of these challenges can be successfully overcome by the implementation of a holistic and systematic approach toward companywide maintenance. A total productive maintenance (TPM) system is one powerful tool the maintenance team and the entire factory can employ to expel crisis management in response to unplanned losses of capacity.

Making Order out of Chaos

At one company, where both manufacturing and maintenance fell under my umbrella of responsibility, I was both amazed and frustrated at how a broken CNC milling machine would send our production schedule and company into a tailspin, compromising our ability to deliver products as promised. As we juggled dozens of custom sales orders for fabricated, machined, and assembled capital goods, a machine going down was a real business constraint. Depending on the time required to revive the equipment, commitments to customers could be delayed by days, weeks, or even months as we played catch-up. A second breakdown of another machine (or the same one) meant we were always playing catch-up using overtime—which put an unnecessary burden on employees.

Then, our insightful maintenance manager approached me with a plan. He wanted to remove each CNC machine from the available capacity list every year for a full two-week preventive maintenance overhaul. Though the idea seemed extreme at first, it proved to be worthwhile. It took nearly two years to enjoy the full benefits, but unplanned downtime caused by machine problems began to plummet immediately, and available uptime became a predictable reality.

The data gathered from the two-week service activities also provided critical information for predictive maintenance. Failing components and their remaining lifespan were identified so parts could be replaced before they failed, and the proper intervals for calibrating machines that required more frequent attention were identified as well. The information from the new service plan also created a more coherent lubrication schedule and resulted in a list of defined daily level-one maintenance activities for operators to complete, freeing up some of the technician's time and inviting machine operators to take ownership of the equipment they ran. This dedicated approach also resulted in reducing the time machines were out for service from the original planned two-week period.

Did the activity prevent all unplanned breakdowns? No, but almost. The effort dramatically reduced the frequency and number of machine breakdowns. Original planned capacity was restored with confidence, and this particular cause of unplanned downtime was virtually removed.

We also learned that each piece of equipment had its inherent differences, its own "personality." We found that although different pieces of machinery may have shared the same manufacturer, model, and year built, each exhibited slightly different nuances in performance (ability to hold tolerance, tool and pallet changing, and actual feeds and speeds) as we got to know each better. Clearly, there had been variables in the original processes that produced these machines. In addition, each machine had experienced a completely different workload history and slight differences in foundations and installation, too. No two pieces of machinery performed exactly the same.

The bottom line for the maintenance manager was this: getting control of the maintenance processes and leaving the chaos behind meant easing the work requirements on his team by reducing demand and more effectively delivering preventive, predictive, and repair maintenance to factory equipment.

TOTAL PRODUCTIVE MAINTENANCE—AN OVERVIEW

TPM is a company-wide holistic approach for improving the effectiveness and longevity of machines. The benefits of TPM include the following:

- Reduced downtime
- Reduce breakdown costs
- Reduced spare parts costs
- Reduced defect rate
- Reduced lead times
- Improved on-time deliveries

Any TPM program should include a maintenance plan for each area of responsibility and every piece of manufacturing and support equipment. The TPM schedule represents the three types of TPM—proactive, preventive, and predictive maintenance. The TPM schedule must also include the original equipment manufacturer's (OEM's) recommended service schedule. A visual representation should exist for each TPM project.

All maintenance areas will need to be organized through 5S events. An organized visual management system moves the responsibility of caring for equipment from being solely with the maintenance department to plant-wide participation and accountability.

The Three Approaches to TPM

There are three approaches at the heart of a TPM program:

- Proactive maintenance
- Preventive maintenance
- Predictive maintenance

Proactive Maintenance

The proactive approach involves performing a set of simple to moderate-level checks on a regular basis, including tasks such as the following:

- Checking settings
- Cleaning and inspection
- Lubrication
- Abnormality detection
- Precision checks
- Triage maintenance

Preventive Maintenance

Some items are designed for periodic replacement or adjustment. The preventive approach means setting up a schedule for periodic replacement and adjustment times in the TPM plan. Examples include the following:

- Replacing parts (e.g., belts, filters)
- Replacing and refilling vital fluids (e.g., lubricants, cutting fluids)
- Recalibrating devices
- Developing new standards for preventive maintenance activities (i.e., revising the standards as information is learned from historic performance to improve the PM process)

Predictive Maintenance

The predictive approach relies on collecting data and using OEM recommendations to develop a plan for replacing or refurbishing parts before they break. The types of data to collect and analyze include the following information:

- Status of filters or dust collectors
- Condition of timing belts
- Hours on machine
- Status of air compressor fluid

Predictive maintenance means developing the ability to predict accurately the timing of part replacement or refurbishment for items that go beyond those designed for periodic replacement. For example, load-bearing surfaces often wear out and need repair. A predictive approach would restore the worn surfaces before they reach a state in which nonconforming products could be produced.

The Three Levels of TPM

The TPM system functions at three levels of the organization: production operators, maintenance technicians, and equipment suppliers.

TPM Level 1: Operators

Although not all companies involve operators in performing PM on the equipment they operate, those who do invite operator participation reap tremendous benefits. These maintenance activities are generally easy to perform, and doing so invites operators to become stewards of the equipment. In turn, this practice, known as autonomous maintenance (AM), brings to light machine issues sooner and relieves the maintenance team from some of the daily workload. AM involves work that does not require oversight from the maintenance team, which means machine operators can complete these actions autonomously once they have been trained and certified to do so. Typically, these are tasks that should be performed daily or more frequently and can be done by following a written procedure that covers relatively simple steps. Of course, operators must be allowed sufficient time to perform AM. Normally, the ability to spot signs of trouble early more than makes up for the time required to complete the activity.

The criteria for operator-level preventive maintenance activities are summarized as follows:

- Work should be performed daily or more often.
- Operator can follow a written procedure, posted on the machine, and track completion by signing off with initials and date.
- Frequency for performing tasks is included in the written procedure.
- Tasks are usually simple.
- Operators must be allowed time to perform the maintenance work.
- The maintenance activities performed by operators at companies that have embraced TPM covers a continually growing list of tasks that will help detect signs of trouble early, including activities such as the following:
  - Cleaning equipment
  - Checking fluid levels
  - Checking equipment settings
  - Replenishing vital fluids
- Identifying additional preventive maintenance required for maintenance staff to perform (Level 2).

TPM Level 2: Maintenance Technicians

With operators shouldering some of the PM work, the maintenance team can focus on other preventive, predictive, and proactive activities. Although most machine manufacturers provide a list of recommended PM activities, discriminating users usually find that additional maintenance is necessary to ensure that the machinery continues to perform as desired. These standard PM steps, which, like the AM tasks, are based on a written schedule and a written procedure, are performed less frequently than the AM tasks—weekly, monthly, or annually. They include activities such as the following:

- Machine repairs
- Machine or equipment teardown
- Machine modifications
- Replacing parts

- Work completed during planned downtime
- Assigned projects

The criteria for PM work to be performed at Level 2 are summarized as follows:

- Based on a written frequency.
- Based on a written procedure.
- Documentation is posted on machines.
- Maintenance must keep records, including the time, parts, and frequency required to perform PM activities.
- PM activities are posted and tracked on a visual board.
- Technicians must be cross-trained and cross-training progress tracked visually on a posted matrix.

In this maintenance model, the technician is responsible for posting documentation on or near the machinery and for keeping accurate records. Developing a visual board showing the status of scheduled TPM activities is a key to success. Records kept should include the hours, parts, and frequency required for activities. As when creating a standard time for manufacturing a part, these data allow the maintenance team to see how much time and money to plan for their efforts. Many maintenance teams use database software that gives them a holistic view of a machine's performance over time.

Information gained from Level-2 activities can drive changes to the Level-1 list. Cross-training is recommended for the maintenance technicians, and keeping and posting a cross-training matrix clarifies who is able to perform certain types of work.

TPM Level 3: Equipment Suppliers

Almost every manufacturing company needs to call on an equipment supplier from time to time to help resolve a maintenance issue. When senior management personnel insist that their maintenance team undertake an effort that really should have included the original equipment supplier, the machine's condition will undoubtedly worsen, and the supplier will need to be called in later anyway. A valid need to involve the machinery supplier often occurs, regardless of whether the equipment is under warranty.

In a TPM system, plan on a certain frequency of involvement from suppliers for maintenance on any critical piece of equipment, whether it be a five-axis milling head needing calibration or an exhaust fan requiring an overhaul. These suppliers may be in your plant only once or twice per year, but the information gleaned—along with the work completed—makes it a worthwhile venture.

For larger production equipment, long-term service agreements are often available once the original warranty period has expired. Feedback from equipment suppliers can provide information to update Level-2 (maintenance level) activities and can subsequently reduce offsite support requirements. The criteria for typical vendor activities are summarized as follows:

- Occurs once or twice a year
- Helps in updating Level-2 PM schedules
- Provides offsite support
- Involves major overhauls and replacing equipment

IMPLEMENTING TPM AND TPM VISUALS

Following are the 10 basic steps for implementing a TPM system, along with some tips and key points. This basic list is intended to serve as a quick outline of the process as it relates to visual management:

1. Start by implementing 5S in the maintenance department.
2. Develop a kanban and material replenishment system for the maintenance department and its activities.
3. Identify the equipment to be placed on a TPM schedule.
   a. Select a group of machines in a limited area. It is best to start with a small work area, or family of similar machines, as a learning ground. Definitely do not start with the most complex equipment.
   b. Learn the process. This involves two activities: (1) when scheduling a machine for PM, understand how the process has been performing; and (2) studying and understanding the key elements of the PM process.

4. Conduct an abnormality assessment.
   a. First, identify the current condition of the machines, and create a baseline for each piece of equipment using the following seven types of abnormalities:
      i. Minor flaws, parts, and vital components
      ii. Basic conditions not fulfilled
      iii. Inaccessible places
      iv. Sources of contamination
      v. Sources of quality defects
      vi. Unnecessary items
      vii. Unsafe places or conditions
   b. Next, schedule fixes and upgrades to address abnormalities.
5. Determine operator- and maintenance-level PM activities.
   a. Identify the Level-1 (operator) and Level-2 (maintenance technician) tasks and the frequency with which they should be performed.
   b. Evaluate PM activities on an ongoing basis, and modify as needed. Be sure to continue to shift frequent, routine maintenance tasks to operators as appropriate.
6. Identify the parts, tools, and facility requirements specific to the activities and actions in each work area.
7. Identify training needs for operator and maintenance levels.
   a. Assess the current abilities and needs of all operators and maintenance technicians.
   b. Develop a cross-training matrix based on three levels of expertise:
      i. Trained. There are five progressive steps to being certified as trained:
         (a) Entry level
         (b) Trained on the new TPM activities for the machines selected
         (c) Can perform the TPM activities under supervision
         (d) Given some leeway to perform independently
         (e) After one to two weeks of consistent performance, **certified**
      ii. Certified
         (a) Performs consistently
         (b) Identifies quality errors and reacts properly

(c) Completes a probationary period of 90 days

(d) For further development, either learns TPM activities on another machine or becomes **certified to train**

iii. Certified to train

(a) Has mastered the machines and can train others

8. Develop standard work for both operators and maintenance.

a. To develop the TPM standards, first identify the TPM steps in the order that they should be performed. Then gather the related information, including cycle time requirements, parts and the quantities required, tools needed, and facility needs, if any.

b. Create a TPM standard worksheet to be installed at the point of use, not compiled in a large binder or stored in a cabinet. TPM standard worksheets need to be easily accessible where they will actually be used for training and on-the-job reference. Make them easy to understand by using simple and concise language, employing icons and symbols consistently throughout, and including computer-aided design (CAD) drawings or pictures. Be sure that the worksheets are usable by employees who may be colorblind or by those for whom English is a second language.

9. Develop visual TPM boards for machines (Figure 6.1). Visual TPM boards provide visual direction on TPM. Used by both operators and maintenance staff, they serve as a proactive measure and provide a point of accountability for performance. Machine TPM boards should be placed on the actual machines or in the work area and include the following elements:

a. Daily schedule for operators

b. Monthly schedule for maintenance

c. Color coding by shift

d. TPM standard worksheets

e. Visual indicators of machine status (Note that black pin-striping tape works well for making the gridlines.)

10. Develop a TPM schedule board for the maintenance department. The maintenance department needs its own TPM schedule board to provide a visual guideline for the TPM schedule and to reduce cherry picking of responsibilities. All maintenance staff must be cross-trained, as discussed further in the section that follows.

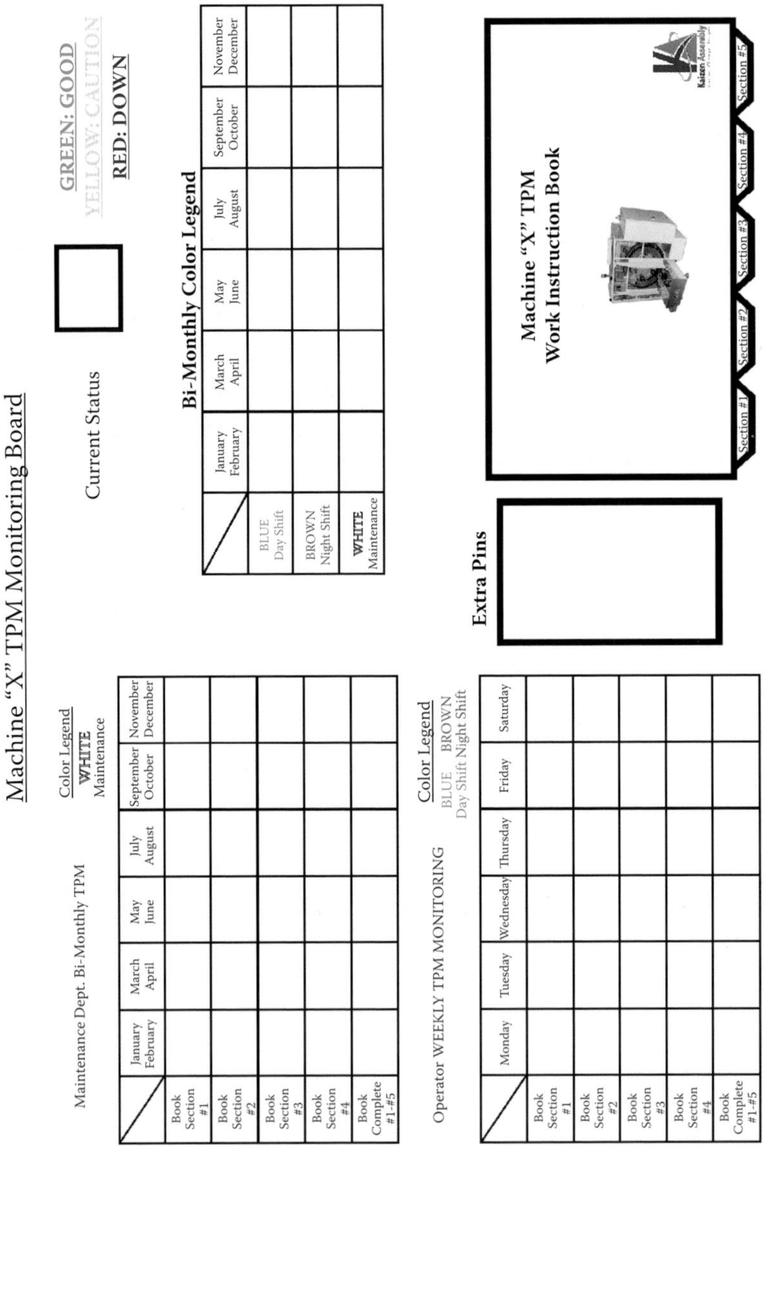

Machine "X" TPM Monitoring Board

GREEN: GOOD
YELLOW: CAUTION
RED: DOWN

Current Status

Bi-Monthly Color Legend

	January February	March April	May June	July August	September October	November December
BLUE Day Shift						
BROWN Night Shift						
WHITE Maintenance						

Machine "X" TPM
Work Instruction Book

Kaizen Assembly

Section #1 Section #2 Section #3 Section #4 Section #5

Extra Pins

Maintenance Dept. Bi-Monthly TPM

Color Legend
WHITE
Maintenance

	January February	March April	May June	July August	September October	November December
Book Section #1						
Book Section #2						
Book Section #3						
Book Section #4						
Book Complete #1-#5						

Operator WEEKLY TPM MONITORING

Color Legend
BLUE   BROWN
Day Shift Night Shift

	Monday	Tuesday	Wednesday	Thursday	Friday	Saturday
Book Section #1						
Book Section #2						
Book Section #3						
Book Section #4						
Book Complete #1-#5						

FIGURE 6.1
Visual TPM board.

Maintenance staff can identify the next TPM projects, and the supervisor can assign maintenance technicians as needed. Cross-training makes it much easier to schedule around vacations and absences.

CROSS-TRAINING

Within the maintenance department it is typical to find individuals with specific and dedicated areas of expertise. For example, not everyone has the qualifications to be a certified electrician. Likewise, a certified electronic technician may struggle with a mechanical repair. When a maintenance team is made up of "subject experts," more personnel, and therefore more overhead costs, may be required to resource projects and implement preventive maintenance measures. The personal interests of some individuals can make cross-training in new areas difficult. Yet in the name of helping the team and company achieve a higher level of competitiveness, especially in the current economy, employees willing to stretch beyond their comfort zone will increase their own value to the company and will reduce the need for the company to employ additional people.

As mentioned previously, one way to visually communicate and track the ability and expertise of each technician is by using a capability matrix (Figure 6.2).

Maintenance Team Matrix								
Level 1	Level 1	Level 1	Level 2	Level 2	Level 2	Level 3	Level 3	Level 3
Mechanical	Electrical	Electronic	Mechanical	Electrical	Electronic	Mechanical	Electrical	Electronic
Name								
John	X	X	X	X	X	X	X	X	X
Luiz	X	X	X	X	X			X	
Kim	X	X	X	X			X		
Ryan	X	X			X				

FIGURE 6.2
Maintenance cross-training matrix.

VISUAL LAYOUT FOR THE MAINTENANCE AREA

As with any work area, we need to understand the key processes occurring within the maintenance area and create a layout that will best accommodate these activities.

In a typical maintenance area (before 5S), we find various sizes and locations of workbenches. Shelving is randomly stocked with repair parts, rebuilt units, hand tools, and assorted bins with nuts, bolts, and fittings. Hoses, tires, and belts hang randomly on the walls, and the area is littered with obsolete parts, broken pieces, and overflowing trash bins. Tool chests and cabinets are of different sizes and colors. Oftentimes, lighting is poor.

One unique aspect of a maintenance operation is that work can take place within the maintenance area, which we refer to as the common area, or on the production floor, or both. It may not seem that important, but dealing with multiple work locations creates certain challenges. Add to that the mix of internal customers making visits to (and demands on) the maintenance team area and summoning maintenance technicians to the factory floor, and it is easy to see that the maintenance operation requires a distinct protocol.

Creating a visual layout for maintenance is quite similar to doing so for production. Apply what you learned about 5S in Chapter 2, starting with clearly marking off floor items with distinct designations and address identifications. Figures 6.3 and 6.4 show examples of 5S implementation and visual layout in a maintenance department.

Creating a Common Area

A maintenance common area is dramatically different from an operator workstation. While production operations have a repetitive need for tools and materials supporting their value-adding operation, the common area provides for more discrete, one-of-a-kind events (i.e., projects and repairs). In addition, common areas support multiple locations throughout the factory, whereas the production maintenance area is typically focused on a specific operation or work area.

The amount of maintenance tools and supplies to be located in the maintenance common area should be based on actual use. This area should be adequately lit and as secure as necessary in keeping with the nature of the

FIGURE 6.3
Visual maintenance layout.

business and the company culture. In smaller companies where there is a less formal atmosphere and a high trust level, all tools are usually available to whoever needs them whenever they are needed. At the opposite extreme, all tools and equipment are kept under lock and key in a tool cage with access only through a formal checkout system.

Tools, Equipment, and Consumables Storage

When it does not make fiscal sense to purchase multiples of certain maintenance tools and supplies, the common area provides a great home base from which items can be shared. Tool boards and kanban bins should be used in the common area to provide a visual snapshot of what item is where and to enhance the immediate availability of a desired tool. No hand tool, gauge, fixture, or power tool should be stored directly on the floor. (See Chapter 4 for details on the creation and use of tool boards.)

In addition, equipment such as shop milling machines, metal lathes, metal or wood band saws or a table saws, or welding machines may simply need a secure and safe area to operate. And the cost of installing utilities

FIGURE 6.4
Visual maintenance layout, close-up.

(hard-wired electrical power, compressed air, or vacuum ducting) may prohibit making equipment available in more than one location. Each piece of equipment should have a home that is marked off on the floor, and any applicable safety or work instructions must be made visible.

Another major group of items requiring storage in the common area is the consumables: lubricants of every kind, including organic and synthetic fluids, hand towels, hand cleaners, replacement parts (e.g., filters, seals, belts, and bulbs), equipment-specific items, and safety items. When it comes to storing items in the common area, consideration should be given to frequency of use, weight and size, distance to the point of use, and time to replace the consumable.

Measurement and Calibration Equipment

When it comes to verification and calibration instrumentation, the story is similar. It may not be cost-effective to purchase multiple CNC axis calibration ball–bar units and the supporting software, yet it may make perfect sense to have multiple sets of digital calipers on hand. Having one oscilloscope in the shop may suffice, but how many torque wrenches are needed? Bring the team together, and have a candid discussion before submitting a tool purchase budget.

No matter how the decision is made on how many of each item should be located in the common area, it is critical to ensure that a shortage of one tool does not result in unplanned loss of capacity for production equipment. Problems often surface in the form of insufficient measurement equipment. However, this is not an area to skimp on. Keep in mind that as manufacturers are increasingly being driven to proactively show that their processes are capable of producing parts to specification, there is a growing need to quantify machine capability to operate within an acceptable range (e.g., tolerances, cutting speed, spindle speeds, tool change time, mixing accuracy, colors). For larger companies, the need to report statistical process control information, including a process capability (Cpk) number, may be paramount prior to being awarded a contract. In addition, discriminating customers, especially those with pending government contracts or rigid tolerance requirements, value the merits of applied statistical methods and often include them as part of the contract specification. They will want to understand the scope of the company's quality program, to establish a baseline for future comparison, and to require that statistical data accompany each shipment. The evolving maintenance technician will have a thorough understanding of process capability and control concepts for production equipment and will be well versed in interpreting both types of data.

As a part of the visual factory, process capability and process control data are measured and reported visually. Why would we want to post a machine's capability and process control data? This critical information should be visual because as variables change—due to wear on axis drives and ways, failing control components, and other aspects of machine operation—everyone can see the changes in real time. If we measure, post, and act on this information as unfavorable trends develop, we can catch a problem before nonconforming products appear.

A point worth noting here has to do with operations in which separate pieces of equipment constitute an equipment group or workcell; if one piece of equipment goes down, production stops for all machines. In these cases, maintaining capacity for each piece of equipment is paramount, and it is even more critical to have quantifiable and real-time information regarding key operational variables. It is bad enough when one machine goes down, let alone more than one. Making workcell and production line performance data visible on the project board helps everyone see the ongoing status.

As with items in the common area, measurement and calibration devices need a home for storage; both the item and the storage location should be visibly labeled. As is the case with equipment that is sensitive to heat, moisture, and airborne particulates, an appropriate clean storage location may be required. Even in these instances, visibility through a sealed window provides the same effect as a tool mounted on a shadow board.

Common Area Layout

In addition to serving as a storage area for maintenance tools, equipment, and consumables, the common area is also the location at which various maintenance activities occur. To size up the space required for these activities, start by counting the number of workbenches and tabletops. Next, count how many are simply acting as a flat storage space and have little room for anyone to work. Most maintenance areas start with too many workbenches and tabletops. Proper determination of how many work surfaces are necessary should be driven not by the number of maintenance technicians but rather by the type and frequency of work being done. In addition, with capacity decisions being risk decisions, the maintenance manager will need to determine the amount of required work surfaces needed. Workbenches are not proper storage locations in the visual factory. They should be used for actual work and should be brightly lit.

Many maintenance teams do their best to organize their work area. Many layouts, however, seem to remain two-dimensional, minimizing the use of vertical space. Even where we do use vertical space, the density of storage is seldom optimal.

As on the production floor, all tools and equipment needed to support the genuine workbench activity should be set in order and be close at hand to promote the flow of work. Tool boards are a great resource in the common work area.

Maintenance Layout on the Production Floor

In addition to the common area, oftentimes we need to organize space on the production floor for maintenance support. Depending on the frequency and severity of support requirements, more than one remote maintenance location may be required. These areas may have their own tool boards for immediate access to tools and visual boards showing machine status (if such information cannot be located right on the equipment). A well-designed tool cart is a handy way to provide machine-specific maintenance areas with a readily available set of tools and parts. Akin to a tool belt around one's waist, the tool cart is designed to accommodate frequently used tools and equipment. It minimizes the number of trips back and forth to the maintenance area, thereby reducing the amount of time a machine is down for maintenance. Oftentimes, miniature tool boards are affixed right to the tool cart, making it even easier to retrieve an item.

Maintenance 5S

After a successful 5S activity as described in Chapter 2, each maintenance area should be organized with tools, equipment, and locations for everything labeled. Each item is stored in a manner that promotes the flow work in both the maintenance common area as well as where the tools are actually used near a machine. It should take technicians less time to find tools, giving them more time to conduct their important work. Normally, the only item that remains unchanged after a 5S event is the clock.

Visual Tool Boards

As described in detail in Chapter 4, tool boards are important in production areas and are also needed to support maintenance activities.

We need to determine not only the location of maintenance tool boards within the facility but also where tools will go on each board. A location for each tool is meticulously selected with tool weight and human reach in mind. Not only the tool but also the location where it hangs are labeled, providing a link between tool and storage location. Figures 6.5 and 6.6 show examples of the application of visual tool boards in maintenance departments.

Personal Tools

We explored some issues related to the use and organization of personal tools in Chapter 4. Regarding maintenance departments, specifically, some companies have found good reason to provide all maintenance tools to their workers simply due to the floor space freed up by removing personal tool chests.

FIGURE 6.5
Large maintenance tool board.

If it is company policy for maintenance personnel to have their own set of tools and equipment, be sure to factor in the need to comply with the company's calibration system. The bottom line is to keep all tools, whether personal or company owned, identified and calibrated with a legitimate calibration sticker. Calibration stickers are a part of the visual management system. Anyone can tell at a glance when, where, and by whom the item was checked.

Name Tags

Another step in organizing the maintenance common area is to provide color-coded name tags for each maintenance technician. These name tags satisfy the need for the LOCK OUT/TAG OUT portion of the safety system, and they are also useful to hang on the tool board where a tool was removed for use. The tag indicates who removed a tool from the tool board or tool bin, who cut the power to a machine, who is on duty, and who is off. The use of the tags takes the guesswork out of locating both people and tools and provides better accountability for everyone.

FIGURE 6.6
Small maintenance tool board.

MAINTENANCE CONSUMABLES AND KANBAN

As with production, the maintenance team "consumes" purchased product and raw materials for projects and machine preservation and repair. Although not intended for use in saleable products, these items are used in support of plant and equipment projects, repairs, and operation.

For HVAC filters, nuts and bolts, project paint, and similar supplies, an effective kanban system, complete with kanban cards and defined inventory quantities and inventory locations, is a very important visual tool to aid in maintaining the correct amount of maintenance supplies while never running out. Another scheme that can, for select commodities, complement the in-house kanban system is to make the nuts-and-bolts or fitting supplier responsible for providing the bins and for carrying the inventory in your factory, leaving you to pay only for the floor space to house the bins and for what you actually use. Regardless of who maintains the inventory, all items must be clearly marked and their consumption recorded for the purposes of efficient replenishment.

We establish quantities based on demand and availability. Once periodic consumption is known, calculating demand is straightforward. We recommend keeping inventories low—but keep enough on hand to support the repair of production equipment. Separate parts into the following categories:

- High
  - High probability of demand
  - Very expensive to replace
  - Long lead time to procure
- Medium
  - Average probability of demand
  - Moderate cost to replace
  - Predictable lead time to procure
- Low
  - Low probability of demand
  - Low cost to replace
- Short lead time to purchase

From this matrix we can create a thumbnail calculation of how many of each component to keep on hand. Another aspect of the calculation is the vendor's minimum order quantity. Wherever possible, we suggest the minimum order quantity be renegotiated to a number that better reflects your need rather than your vendor's need. Agreeing to accept a minimum order quantity to achieve the lowest per-unit price may satisfy short-sighted accounting needs, but it also requires carrying more inventory than what is needed. That means carrying inventory that may never be used, that will become obsolete, and that will eventually be written off.

As items are consumed, we will reach a point to reorder. Using a visual system for reorder is the key, as described in Chapter 5. In summary, when an item is pulled to meet demand it exposes a red dot, which means it is time to reorder. All the inventory calculations are transparent to the person picking the parts by virtue of the visual factory system. Of course, these parts-on-hand numbers may need to be massaged and recalculated if you lack good numbers to start with or if a significant process change occurs due to a change in market demand, equipment reliability, or part availability.

OVERALL EQUIPMENT EFFECTIVENESS

Any discussion of the role of maintenance in a visual factory would not be complete without mentioning the concept of overall equipment effectiveness (OEE). OEE calculations look at the relationships among availability, performance, and quality for each piece of equipment, workcell, or production line, and each gets a scorecard. The role of maintenance is visible within the availability and performance numbers.

Proactive and analytical maintenance managers will want to better understand the OEE calculation and how it is used and will post the information as a part of the visual management system.

THE MAINTENANCE MANAGER

Now that both the maintenance common area and all individual remote maintenance areas are in place, secure, and organized, how does this help maintenance managers, who have been operating in chaos? With a foundation in place, they can ratchet up their ability to become more proactive, predictive, and aggressive with maintenance activities.

With a TPM program in place, they can respond better with preventive maintenance steps to reduce equipment breakdowns. As breakdowns do occur, they are better prepared with readily available tools and the know-how to respond. Posting machine information allows them to see a potential problem before it occurs and provides an opportunity for operators to assist in seeing unfavorable trends before a bad part is made. Posted information shows what Level-1 PM work has been performed. Technicians are being cross-trained and are recording the status of each piece of equipment and collecting quantifiable breakdown data. Management has backed off a bit to give them some breathing room. They have a workable plan. In essence, their entire team has been completely refocused to concentrate on its original purpose.

7

Visual Communications

As you probably understand by now, visual control is about having what you need to perform your value-added work more effectively with better quality. A visual layout is conducive to overall visibility of all consuming processes and supporting departments. Tools and material must be nearby and visible for immediate retrieval. Everything is kept in a state of impeccable organization that creates an environment of discipline.

Often, manufacturing professionals forget the importance of visual information and communication. One of the biggest creators of wasted motion and waiting is not having the proper information when necessary. In other cases, the information may be readily available, but it contains administrative errors that create manufacturing problems or add to waste when people need to be pulled from their jobs for correction or clarification.

This book is all about visual communication. Implementation of 5S is ultimately about creating a workplace that communicates the status of all activities visually. Color-coded work areas quickly communicate when the wrong item is out of place. Designated addresses on tools visually communicate the location to which tools should be returned. Kanban cards visually communicate ordering procedures and home locations of bins, parts, supplies, and material. Visual control in all its glory is about communication.

This chapter is dedicated to describing the importance of visual communication of the performance, goals, and objectives necessary to support a visual factory. It covers the following items:

- Facility performance
- Metrics communication boards at the production level
- Production control boards
- Communication lights
- Lean procedures

FACILITY PERFORMANCE

One of the key functions of visual communication is to relay important company information to the entire facility. Often, manufacturers have multiple facilities throughout the country or even the world. Try to keep the information specific to the facility so that there is a direct connection for the plant employees who are affecting performance. This does not imply that overall corporate performance is irrelevant; that type of information can be conveyed in some other form of communication.

First, your plant needs to decide what information it makes sense to communicate. Some executives keep performance information out of sight of employees, because they are reluctant to communicate bad information like reduced orders, poor deliveries, or poor sales. To be honest, this is exactly what should be communicated. Obviously, we prefer information to be positive, but showing performance trends is healthy. Here are the company metrics that should be communicated visually on a company communication board in places like break rooms:

- Sales
- On-time delivery (OTD)
- Productivity
- Quality
- Safety
- Environment

Sales

Ongoing communication of sales information is very smart. Employees can see how well the products they touch and build every day are moving into the hands of consumers. As sales increase, the plant will gain encouragement that the revenue stream is growing. On the other hand, a decrease in sales is equally important to communicate to employees. The purpose of this category is to show trends so that everyone can get a sense of the money coming in. Your challenge is to decide how much sales information to post visibly in community areas like break rooms. Regardless of your approach, sales information is at the top of the list. Sales dollars or units sold can be the measure.

On-Time Delivery

Plant performance on OTD must be communicated on the same board. This metric can be a little tricky when some plants tout 100% on-time delivery, but the reason for achieving such a high percentage is excessive finished-goods inventory resulting from overproduction. Of course, this does not imply that you should shoot for a 70% OTD. First, decide how you will measure OTD. Consider the following questions: Do you consider a product to be delivered as soon as it leaves the facility or when it shows up on the customer's receiving dock? Are you responsible for the shipping method and timing? Do you constantly change the delivery date because of engineering changes? Once you decide on how you want to measure, stick with one delivery date as the mark you shoot for. The metric to use is on-time delivery percentage, and an industry performance of 92% is a good mark.

Productivity

The next metric to communicate is plant-wide productivity. This metric reflects the productivity of every individual work area, workcell, or assembly line in a cumulative score of overall plant efficiency. Like any metric, the selection of the measurable is important. Productivity can be measured in a variety of ways, such as labor dollars per unit, the distance product travels per person, pound per machine, or bags per person.

Productivity is improving when products are manufactured with less effort, fewer workers or hours, less equipment, and less use of utilities (overhead). If you are using labor dollars per unit, you are essentially measuring your ability to overproduce. Are those units you are making and measuring at labor dollars per unit headed straight to the finished goods shelf where they will sit until an order comes in? A better productivity measurement is sales per head count or labor dollars per unit sold. Regardless, like all the items on your facility performance board, you should show the current rate of productivity and recent trends.

Quality

Quality is another key measurable for a factory. Surprisingly, we have come across companies that do not measure quality, which is a big mistake. Quality should be measured internally and externally, because there truly is a difference. Internal measurements of quality could include defective parts per million (PPM), rework hours, rejects, scrap, or nonconformances. External measurements of quality include customer complaints, warranty claims, cost of resolution, and cost of service calls. It is best to communicate both internal and external quality information to everyone on your communication board.

Safety

To start, favorable safety results are driven more by a culture that promotes an attitude of safety than by expectations for compliance with company safety policy and regulatory mandates. Either way, a manufacturing company's safety goal is normally to provide a safe workplace where all employees and visitors are free from the danger of incidents or injuries. Whereas an incident may be considered a near miss, an accident is an event in which someone is injured or killed. The impact to both the employer and the employee can be catastrophic. Company leaders who find ways to create a culture that supports an attitude of safety will benefit everyone.

Whether a report is required to be posted, sharing information regarding accidents and incidents is a healthy contributor to the visual factory. Following are some items to report:

- Accident-free days
- Costs of lost work days
- Number of accidents
- Number of incidents
- Hazardous material storage compliance reports
- Fire inspection reports
- Corrective actions taken to remove causes of incidents and accidents

Posting these reports will help raise the awareness of employees who read them, but ultimately ongoing training and positive reinforcement are required to maintain and increase the importance of working safely in everyone's mind.

Environmental

Environmentally unfriendly practices are more than a regulatory concern; society no longer accepts such practices. Communicating compliance with federal, state, and local laws as well as other aspects of environmental performance reinforces your company's commitment to the workforce and to society as a whole.

Examples to share proactively may include the following:

- Emission test results
- Drainage test reports
- Airborne particulate levels
- Facility heat loss
- Fleet fuel usage
- Recycling efforts
- Employee use of public transportation

Communicate environmental performance (rather than just compliance) in a way that invites employee participation.

METRICS COMMUNICATION BOARDS AT THE PRODUCTION LEVEL

It is important to take the concept of the facility performance communication board down to the production and departmental level. Communication boards that visually depict the performance of individual work areas should be constructed and placed in each work area. Although it is important to know and improve on plant-wide OTD, for example, the plant-wide OTD metric does not necessarily help an individual work area improve its own OTD.

Metrics at the work area or cell level must be relevant to that area. What is the area's productivity and quality? What is the goal for output and delivery to the next process? For example, if a product is partially manufactured in cell 1 and then has to travel and be processed in three more areas, the plant-wide OTD metric does not help cell 1 assess its own OTD percentage. Instead, use the work-in-process date (WIP) date for a given work area. When is it due to the next consuming process? That is the immediate internal customer.

When developing area or departmental metrics boards, try to keep them as standard as possible so that each one conveys the same set of metrics. We recommend the following information:

FIGURE 7.1
Workcell communication board.

- WIP OTD
- Productivity
- Quality
- Safety
- Attendance
- 5S Scores

Figure 7.1 shows an example that displays these metrics.

Metrics communication boards are used to constantly monitor performance and to provide information that drives future improvements. While it may be hard for individual employees to take ownership of plant-wide rework hours, they can more easily take ownership of the rework hours in their own work areas.

PRODUCTION CONTROL BOARDS

Imagine yourself as a coach on a football field. During each quarter of a football game, coaching requires constant decision making and the

Time	Required	Actual	Difference	Current	Comments
9:00	10	10	0	10	N/A
10:00	10	8	−2	18	Tool Broke
11:00	10	11	+1	29	N/A
12:00	10	10	0	39	

FIGURE 7.2
Production control board.

creation of plays that will drive the team to score and ultimately to win the game. Every game is coached on a per-play basis, and you want to avoid going into overtime at the end of the game, as that will fatigue the players and may precipitate decisions that are not part of your standard playbook. Imagine how difficult it would be to coach a game without a scoreboard to help guide your decisions and steer your team toward success. Every decision is based on the current situation or status, with the overall objective of winning. Your shop is no different. Each day, you and your people must make decisions to ensure that the work is done in time for the customer pick-up.

Production control boards can be one of the most valuable management tools for increasing output. Of course, to be effective, the information on the board must be accurate—but, when it is, the results are absolutely awesome. A production control board monitors production progress with real-time information, allowing everyone to see whether the process is producing the required amount of work. To illustrate, let's think about an assembly operation, where the line is required to produce 10 widgets per hour and the associated takt time has been set to accommodate that. Figure 7.2 illustrates this idea.

As you can see, assembly progress is monitored hourly, and current information is displayed. If the required output is not being met, you can see this on an hourly basis—not just at the end of the day, when it is too late to do anything about it. Assembly plants have also used takt time to monitor progress by counting how often a widget would have to come off the line—whatever makes sense for each company and process. Each production control board must be designed for the needs of each process—a single template applicable to any and all processes does not exist. A simple dry-erase board will do nicely for most purposes.

Another somewhat different example of how a production control board is applied in a body shop is shown in Figure 7.3. This body shop control board works very well. One shop in Nebraska displays this board on a projector so that everyone can view it, update it, and use it as a guideline. It functions much like a scoreboard. Columns include a place to identify the automobiles currently in the shop and those still parked outside.

This particular board includes the estimating process as well as teardown, prep, paint, reassembly, and detail. It also includes a column to show whether the job is complete, the scheduled pick-up day, and a column for comments or "issues." This particular example is based on the day of the week, in this case, December 15. There are a Dodge, a Honda, a Toyota, a Ford, and a Jeep in the "system." For each car, a promised pick-up date is identified in the due date column. Green represents where the car needs to be in the shop, based on the pick-up date. Red represents where the car is in relation to that date—only if it is behind schedule. A car with one green column means that it is on schedule and is currently in the correct process. Two green columns mean that the car is actually ahead of schedule. In this example, the Dodge is on schedule in the teardown process, as planned. The Honda should be in paint, but it is still in prep, which means it is behind schedule. The Toyota is completed and ahead of schedule, since it should have been in detail.

	Production Control Board (12–15–2009)								
Car	Estimate	Teardown	Prep	Paint	Re-assemble	Detail	Complete	Due	Issues
Dodge								Monday	
Honda								Monday	Parts
Toyota								Wednesday	
Ford								Thursday	Office
Jeep								Thursday	

FIGURE 7.3
Body Shop Production Control Board.

A production control board is a marvelous visual control tool that technicians can use to flex workers in and out of work areas, maintaining flow and takt time, as discussed in the previous section. As technicians complete their work in an area, they simply update the board and begin working on the next car.

Returning to the football example, as the coach of your shop, you must have a scoreboard that will help you make appropriate decisions and develop strategies to ensure success and avoid being late for a delivery or a pick-up while not incurring overtime, which is something all good coaches wish to avoid.

COMMUNICATION LIGHTS

Communication lights are a critical aspect of visual control. They are quite common even in a facility not practicing all the elements of visual control. These lights are the visual communication system between operators and the rest of the plant. A variety of different styles is available, as shown in Figure 7.4. Choose the type that makes sense for your plant. The most common type of light used in visual control applications consists of three different colored lights—red, yellow, and green—each conveying a specific meaning.

FIGURE 7.4
Communication lights.

Defining what each color means is up to you, but the most common uses are described as follows. Red signals to everyone that a major problem has occurred. Possible reasons to turn on the red light:

- Machine down
- Out of parts
- Tool broke
- High quantity of defective parts

Ideally, the red light should never come on if all the visual control pieces described in this book are in place to give you early warnings that a deviation from the standard is coming. However, it does happen. When the red light goes on, it should be considered a major issue and reacted to immediately.

Yellow communicates that a potential problem is coming but that the process appears to be in control at the moment. Perhaps a machine is acting oddly or making funny sounds that mean a breakdown is coming. Perhaps, even though the kanban card or empty bin from the two-bin system was submitted, material and parts are getting down to uncomfortably low levels. The yellow light can also be turned on if the production control board shows that the process is slowly getting behind schedule. The yellow light is a proactive light to be used ahead of time and hopefully to avoid a major issue that would require red-light initiation.

Green means all is well. No problems need to be reported. Output, quality, material, machines, people, and tools are all working properly, and everything is on track for optimal performance. The visibility achieved from a properly operated communication light system is profound. Managers, operators, and support staff can look across the factory at any moment and see whether the plant is in control. The amount of time and effort wasted in a factory just getting a hold on the status of operations boggles the mind. Production control boards and communication lights, convey that information instantly, as do all visual control tools.

LEAN PROCEDURES

Most people do not think of procedures, assembly instructions, and other production-related documentation as information that needs to be made visual. As far as we are concerned, it is an absolute requirement in the

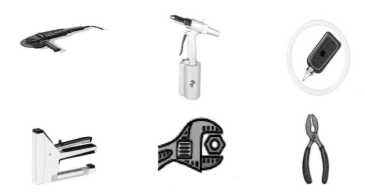

FIGURE 7.5
Procedure icons and symbol.

visual control world. There are many flaws in traditional approaches to procedures. First, procedures often contain information that is not needed at the point of use. Providing too much (i.e., irrelevant) information in instructions is like having too many tools in the work area. Sifting through information to find what is needed is just like sifting through tools to find the right one. It wastes time, money, and resources, and causes frustration.

Procedures of any kind must be developed and presented in a way that makes them easy to understand and follow. If your procedures are wordy and full of irrelevant information, bound in a book, and placed in a cabinet, they are by no means visual, and we can guarantee they are not being used—period. The best way to present simplified procedures is to use icons, symbols, and pictures to explain the work required.

Differing opinions on the purpose and use of procedures have always been around. We believe they serve two essential purposes. The first is to train new employees. That does not imply that you hand a new operator a procedure and say, "Good luck." Rather, documented procedures should be used as a guideline to show the best practice of the area. The second purpose is to serve as a reference and for ongoing accountability. Figure 7.5 shows a few examples of icons and symbols that can be used to illustrate action and keep procedures Lean and simple.

It is also important that Lean procedures be placed at the point of use where the work is performed—not hidden in a cabinet collecting dust. Quick and timely access to relevant and correct information is a vital component of visual control.

Conclusion

In this book, you have read arguments as to why your company could benefit by implementing a visual management system. You have been introduced to a plethora of visual control concepts and examples and ways to make them work. You have recognized the vast use of visual communication in normal daily activities, and we suspect you will now begin to view road signs, crosswalks, stoplights, emergency signs, and other visual indicators (signs, symbols, floor markings, and placards) a bit differently. We imagine that you will begin to look at the use of visual controls within your manufacturing facilities differently, too—in a simpler and more systematic way.

A visual communication system is intended to assist all company employees as they fulfill their respective roles in support of producing value-added products more effectively. From work-zone color coding to posted company-wide metrics, every aspect of visual control is intended to simplify with a clear message. Kanban systems signal when materials need to be reordered; the visual layout of a facility allows for eye contact between workers; and shadow boards provide an organized and instant indicator on the location of every tool. Each concept is designed to eliminate, or at least to significantly reduce, waste in one or more of its eight forms and to provide for a more productive and a safer work environment.

The expected bottom-line impact of reducing waste is easy to understand:

- Lower costs to produce
- Higher first-pass quality rates
- Less need to carry inventory (in its three forms)
- The ability to reduce the time it takes to fill a customer's order

A well-conceived visual management system can prove invaluable in helping achieve these objectives.

Yet a visual management system is still only a tool; it will work well only when it is properly designed to fit your particular manufacturing operation. And, to be of any value, the system must be used and maintained as intended. We understand that many companies simply lack a culture that has matured enough to sustain such an endeavor. These are the companies whose metaphorical crosswalks still lack any visible means of control. System success is only as great as the level at which your management team embraces the concepts and your company culture sustains it. If company leaders create a culture that encourages employee involvement and also fosters a mind-set of continuous improvement, you will have a good chance of success.

When applied correctly, visual signals do help reduce waste, improve communication, and simplify work throughout the factory. Considering such potential, it is amazing that more North American manufacturing companies have not taken advantage of the opportunity to implement comprehensive visual management systems with their relevant visual controls. Where we find companies who are on the path to do so, we find viable production operations with waste being wringed out of processes and skillful workers demonstrating pride of ownership for each process they manage.

Enjoy your Lean journey!

Glossary

5s: A systematic approach to cleaning and organization of a work area. The 5Ss are sort, set in order, shine or scrub, standardize, and sustain.

5s audit sheet: A form used to assess and document how well an area is maintaining the standard established during the last 5S event.

5s event: A planned kaizen activity for implementing 5S in a designated area.

5S supply box: A box used to house all the items necessary to support a kaizen 5S event.

8 wastes: Overproduction, inventory, motion, overprocessing, transportation, waiting, defects, human potential.

Addressing: A Lean term used to describe a method of designating specific locations in a facility (e.g., on the factory floor, on a wall, or on a tool board).

Andon: A type of indicator placed at a machine or work area indicating the operational status of the process.

Changeover: See Setup.

CNC: Computer numerical controlled; typically refers to a machine's controller.

Collection team: Members of a 5S event team whose job is to receive red-tagged items from the sorting team.

Common area: An area set aside for a common use.

Current state: A document showing the current state of a process.

Defects: One of the eight wastes; also referred to as scrap or rejects—suggesting the time and materials taken to make a defect is wasted.

Eco: Engineering change order; controlled information communicating change to an engineering specification. Normally, a description of the change outlined along with a list of all affected products, work orders, and inventoried items.

Effectivity: The notion of when something becomes effective or active.

Equipment: Any equipment, machine, or machinery used in any manufacturing process.

First-time pass rate: A quality system term depicting the rate of conforming parts compared with the total items at the first point of verification (e.g., 99.9% first pass rate).

Future state: Once data have been collected, a future state of the production process can be predicted, calculated, drawn, and implemented.

Hidden factory: Indicates the full cost of manufacturing, including all the costs that are difficult to "account" and are estimated and lumped together. The introduction of myriad Lean concepts and methods has made these costs visible.

Human potential: One of the eight wastes; the underuse of the skills, talents, and thinking ability of employees. Also, having the wrong people in a job.

Inventory: One of the eight wastes, which comes in three basic forms: raw material, work in process (WIP), and finished goods. Inventory levels that exceed what is needed to support all value-adding processes and support activities are considered a waste-reduction opportunity.

Kaizen: A word of Japanese origin meaning "improvement" that has been adopted to represent "continuous improvement."

Kaizen event: An event with a stated purpose to improve an area within the facility.

Kaizen team: A group selected to participate as a team during a kaizen event.

Kanban: A Japanese term that refers to the concept of using a "signal" to simplify communication. These signals are used for material replenishment in production floor, maintenance, and support functions.

Kanban card: A "signal" card used to communicate the need to reorder an item. Includes part identifier, reorder quantity, and both production and inventory location.

Lean manufacturing: Lean manufacturing is a methodology for removing the inefficiencies called "waste." It is a business philosophy of continuous improvement to better satisfy the customer and to become more competitive.

Lean practitioner: An individual who teaches Lean basic and advanced concepts and methods and helps companies organize their Lean initiatives and implement a Lean culture in their facilities.

Master production schedule (MPS): A macro view of projected production demand based on such elements as the sales forecast, actual orders, and scheduled projects.

Materials function: The company role of sourcing, storing, and delivering all purchased materials, parts, subcomponents, consumables, tools, and so forth.

Metric: A variable that is measured.

Motion: One of the eight wastes. Human motion is waste when a worker must move outside of the normal workspace for any reason to support the demands of production.

Nonconforming: A quality term; an item is nonconforming when any aspect (qualitative or quantitative) is not within the documented specification.

On-time delivery (OTD): A metric of delivery performance (e.g., 98.6% OTD).

Overall equipment effectiveness (OEE): These calculations report how well production is performing based on three metrics: availability, performance, and quality. Total effective equipment performance considers the impact of loading on OEE.

Overprocessing: One of the eight wastes; time spent adding more features to a part than what was specified.

Overproduction: One of the eight wastes; when more parts are produced than what are needed to fulfill demand.

Red tag: During 5S events, a red tag is attached to any item sorted out as not needed.

Red-tag area: An area set aside for temporary storage of red-tagged items.

Red-tag register: A list itemizing every item red tagged during a 5S event.

Red-tag removal procedure: A defined procedure for handling items given a red tag during a 5S event.

Reorder point: Within the kanban system, the point at which the signal indicates it is time to reorder a particular item.

Right-sizing: The concept of using only the amount of horizontal or vertical space required to store an item.

Set in order: A 5S term depicting the need to position tools in a way that promotes the flow of work and minimizes wasted motion.

Setup: Reconfiguration of a machine to accommodate a new product. This is a nonvalue-adding process that is normally a prime candidate for waste reduction.

Shadow board: See Tool board.

Shine or scrub: 5S terms capturing the effort to clean up, paint, or add lighting to an area.

Sorting: 5S term capturing the removal of all unnecessary items from a work area.

Sorting team: Members of the 5S team charged with performing the sorting and red-tagging functions.

Standardize: A 5S term pointing to the need to standardize work area procedures.

Sustain: A 5S term suggesting the need and methods to maintain the new state of the process standard.

Takt time: A German word indicating rhythm or rate. Calculated by determining the customer demand for a given product over a certain time period, and the production process is set to run at that rate.

Tool board: A peg board, with peg hooks, which holds tools; an outline (or shadow) is drawn around each tool to define its location on the board.

Tool sequencing: A method of placing tools on a tool board in the sequence in which they will be used.

TPM: Total productive maintenance; a company-wide program ensuring ongoing operation of all equipment.

TPM boards: The maintenance department's visual status of projects and machines.

Travel: One of the eight wastes; pointing to the waste of excessive movement of a part.

Two-bin system: A replenishment system in which parts are pulled from one bin only after a second bin has been emptied; the empty bin serves as the signal to replenish the parts.

Value-added: Adding value suggests process steps a customer is willing to pay for.

Value-added time: The actual manufacturing time used to create value in a product.

Vendor: Entity that sells, distributes, and delivers items considered as "commodities."

Visual communication: Any visual method using for example signs, symbols, colors, charts, or numbers to communicate process information.

Visual factory: A factory using a visual management system, including visual controls and visual communication, throughout all production and support areas.

Visual supplies: A technique for both storing supplies visually and using the kanban approach to make supplies more visible, especially in terms of when to replenish.

Waiting: One of the eight wastes; underscoring the waste (and cost) of having employees or processes waiting before proceeding with value-adding operations.

Work in process (WIP): A form of inventory that represents all stages of value-added products from the time production has commenced until they are completed.

Zone: A work area marked off by color, signage, or signs.

Index

About the Authors

Chris Ortiz is the president and founder of Kaizen Assembly, a Lean manufacturing training and implementation firm in Bellingham, Washington. He has been practicing Lean for over 12 years and speaks around the country at trade shows and manufacturing expositions. He is the author of *Kaizen Assembly: Designing, Constructing, and Managing a Lean Assembly Line* (Taylor & Francis, 2006), *Lessons from a Lean Consultant* (Prentice Hall, 2008), *Kaizen and Kaizen Event Implementation* (Prentice Hall, 2009), and *Lean Auto Body* (Kaizen Assembly, 2009).

Kaizen Assembly has been featured on the show *Inside Business* with Fred Thompson that aired on *CNBC* and *CNN Headline News*. Chris is frequently featured in manufacturing trade magazines including *Industrial Engineer, Industrial Management, Collision Repair Magazine, Metal Finishes, Assembly Magazine*, and dozens of other industry-recognized publications.

He has been trained by the John Costanza Institute of Technology in "Demand Flow Technology" and by the Georgia Institute of Technology for ISO 9001: 2000 Internal Quality Auditing. He is also a member of the Institute of Industrial Engineers and the Society of Manufacturing Engineers.

Murry Park is the founder of MRP ONE, a manufacturing consulting company located in Mount Vernon, Washington. As a 26-year veteran of manufacturing, Murry's service has spanned roles from entry-level engineer to vice president and general manager to senior Lean consultant.

His professional experience includes working with companies from various industries ranging from electronics to metals and aerospace to seafood and from small privately owned companies to larger publicly traded corporations across North America.

Internationally, he has observed and analyzed production processes in Argentina, Belgium, Italy, Japan, and Canada.

Murry's professional experience began in 1983 when volume batch processing was still considered vogue in American manufacturing. However, struggling with the realities of such an approach, he quickly recognized the merits of such new concepts as 5S, setup reduction, one-piece flow, and kanban, as he came to understand and apply them. Seeing immediate and dramatic improvements from every implementation, Murry became a lifelong student—and teacher—in the pursuit of sharing these concepts and methods with others. He has led countless improvement activities and has watched as serious value-adding enterprises embraced a culture of continuous improvement based on employee participation, thereby also enjoying the benefits that followed.